MCQs On Forensic Toxicology

ARCHANA SINGH

Copyright © 2020 Archana Singh

All rights reserved.

ISBN: 9798560500085

MCQs on Forensic Toxicology

First Edition: 2020

© Publisher

Whole book or any part of this book may not be reproduced or modified or transmitted in any form, such as recording, photocopying or copying by any other platform of any type of system whether it is electronic or in offline medium without permission of author of this book.

ISBN: 9798560500085

Price: 1000/-

US $: $13.33

Disclaimer

The author and editor have tried best to provide every information which is true to their knowledge related to the subject. Although author and editor ensure the optimum accuracy of the information and made every effort to retain the right information, yet it may be possible that some errors might have left.

The publisher, the printer, the author and the editor will not be held responsible for any error or inaccuracies.

Description

The "MCQs on Forensic Toxicology" provides access to the questions which have been asked and can be asked in upcoming examinations, such as, NET/JRF, FACT, or other exams in which these subjects are in demand. It consist 500 MCQs on Forensic Toxicology.

This book consists of 500 MCQs of relevant to the Forensic Toxicology. This book will help you to qualify NET/JRF examination as well as other competitive examination related to Forensic Toxicology.

Edited By *@forensicfield*

Contact us:
Contactforensicscience@gmail.com
https://forensicfield.blog/
https://forensicfield.blogspot.com/
https://www.youtube.com/c/ForensicField/
https://www.facebook.com/forensicfield/
https://twitter.com/ForensicField
https://www.instagram.com/forensicfield/
https://www.linkedin.com/in/forensicfield/
https://forensicfield.tumblr.com/

Forensic Toxicology

1. The term Toxicology is derived from the world:

a.) Toxic

b.) Toxicon

c.) Toxico

d.) Toxics

2. The Father of Forensic Toxicology is:

a.) Karl Landsteiner

b.) Amboise Pare

c.) Mathieu J. B. Orfila

d.) Manu

3. The toxicology maxims "*The Dose makes the Poison*" is said by:

a.) Karl Landsteiner

b.) Amboise Pare

c.) Mathieu J. B. Orfila

d.) Paracelsus

4. Study of toxic substance produced by living organism in the human body and their effect is known as:

a.) Toxinology

b.) Toxicology

c.) Forensic Medicine

d.) Clinical Toxicology

5. Any type of natural or synthetic matter/substance which is used to produce physiological and psychological effects in livings is called as:

a.) Poison

b.) Drug

c.) Medicine

d.) Antidote

6. What is the ratio of poison and drug?

a.) 5:10

b.) 2:5

c.) 10:10

d.) 1:10

7. Under NDPS Act following drugs are included, except:

a.) Alcohol

b.) Opium

c.) Amphetamine

d.) Hashish

8. Any substance in any form, is capable of producing detrimental effects on living organism is known as:

a.) Poison

b.) Drug

c.) Medicine

d.) Antidote

9. Which drug is imported under a name of another drug, or it is an imitation of another drug which can deceive the person is known as:

a.) Adulterated Drug

b.) Misbranded Drug

c.) Spurious Drug

d.) Illicit Drug

10. Soluble toxic protein released from gram positive or gram negative bacteria is known as:

a.) Endotoxin

b.) Exotoxin

c.) Enterotoxin

d.) Poison

11. These are heat stable lipopolysaccharide complex of the outer membrane of the cell wall of gram negative bacteria:

a.) Exotoxin

b.) Enterotoxin

c.) Endotoxin

d.) Poison

12. These are toxins produced by bacteria which is specific for intestinal cells:

a.) Exotoxin

b.) Enterotoxin

c.) Endotoxin

d.) Poison

13. Poisoning having Local action only:

a) Sulphuric Acid

b) Arsenic

c) Oxalic Acid

d) Carbon Monoxide

14. Chemicals have specific targets in the body:

a.) Few does have targets, others are nonspecific

b.) Depends on Immune System

c.) Depends on the route of exposure

d.) Chemicals decide after entering into the body

15. Synergism comes from the Greek word, which is:

a.) Synergist

b.) Synerg

c.) Synergos

d.) Antidote

16. A substance which is used to neutralize or counteract the effect of poison is called?

a.) Medicine

b.) Chemical Neutralizer

c.) Antibiotic

d.) Antidote

17. Drugs which are alkaline in nature are called____.

a.) Poison

b.) Alkali

c.) Basic Drug

d.) Acidic Drug

18. Drugs which are acidic in nature are called____.

a.) Poison

b.) Alkali

c.) Basic Drug

d.) Acidic Drug

19. The substance which act chemically to form a nontoxic compound by forming insoluble compounds with the poison are known as-

a.) Universal Antidote

b.) Physiological Antidote

c.) Chemical Antidote

d.) Mechanical Antidote

20. **Universal Antidote for unknown Poison is:**

a.) Powedered Activated Charcoal: Magnesium Oxide: Tannic Acid

b.) Magnesium Oxide: Tinned Juice: Alkalis

c.) Sulphur: Carbolic Acid: Lime

d.) Luke Warm Water

21. **Universal antidote prepared from common household articles:**

a.) Wall Scraping: Tea: Toasted Bread

b.) Soil : Strong Black Tea: Charred Toasted Bread

c.) Wall Scraping: Strong Black Tea: Soap Solution

d.) Wall Scraping: Strong Black Tea: Charred Toasted Bread

22. **The composition of universal antidote includes two parts of:**

a.) Magnesium oxide

b.) Tannic Acid

c.) Powder Activated Charcoal

d.) All of the above

23. Activated Charcoal is an Example for:

a.) Universal Antidote

b.) Physiological Antidote

c.) Chemical Antidote

d.) Mechanical Antidote

24. Activated charcoal is prepared by:

a.) Burning wood

b.) Bacteria

c.) Chemical synthesis

d.) Artificial technique

25. Activated Charcoal is Ineffective in Poisoning of:

a.) Methyl Alcohol

b.) Ethyl Alcohol

c.) Arsenic

d.) All of the above

26. Instead of Charcoal this can be also used:

a.) Raw Egg

b.) Mashed Potatoes in water

c.) Warm Milk

d.) Luke Warm Water

27. Which following poison has no antidote?

a.) Mustard Gas

b.) Hydrofluoric Acid

c.) Batrachotoxin

d.) Sulfur Dioxide

e.) Dimethylmercury

f.) All of the above

28. Atropine and Pralidoxime are antidotes for:

a.) Blood Agent

b.) Nerve Agent

c.) Blister agent

d.) Choking agent

29. In suspected chronic poisoning, the following specimen should be collected:

a.) Hairs

b.) Nails

c.) Skin (sole of feet and palm of hand)

d.) Ends of the long bone.

e.) All of the above

30. A person gets unconscious, excessive salivation, constricted pupils and fasciculation muscles, treatment started with:

a.) Lukewarm water

b.) Atropine

c.) Adrenaline

d.) All of the above

31. All statements are true about symptoms of blister agent, except:

a.) Skin, eye, and mucosal pain and irritation.

b.) Painful breathing or shortness of breath.

c.) Mild respiratory distress to marked airway damage.

d.) Blister agents are denser than air.

32. Following are mineral acids, except:

a.) Sulphuric Acid

b.) Nitric Acid

c.) Hydrochloric Acid

d.) Carbolic Acid.

33. **Which nut contains Cyanide?**

a.) Cashews

b.) Pistachios

c.) Walnuts

d.) Bitter Almonds

34. **PAPP (Para-aminopropiophenone) is used in the treatment of one of the following poison:**

a.) Alcohol poisoning

b.) Barbiturate poisoning

c.) Opiate poisoning

d.) Cyanide poisoning

35. **Which is the most deadly Poison?**

a.) Sulphuric Acid

b.) Arsenic

c.) Botulinum Toxin

d.) Carbon Monoxide

36. **Which Bacteria Produced Botulinum Toxin?**

a.) Streptococcus Pyogenes

b.) Mycobacterium Tuberculosis

c.) Clostridium Botulinum

d.) Acinetobacter Baumannii

37. Botox is known to tighten the skin and reduce wrinkles. Which Toxin is being used in Botox?

a.) Sulphuric Acid

b.) Arsenic

c.) Botulinum Toxin

d.) Carbon Monoxide

38. This is most deadliest poison:

a.) Botulinum Toxin

b.) VX

c.) Maitotoxin

d.) Polonium

e.) All of the above

39. Polonium is a:

a.) Gaseous Element

b.) Liquid Element

c.) solid element

d.) Radioactive Element

40. A potential lethal dose of Polonium-210 is:

a.) 0.1 Sieverts

b.) 10 Sieverts

c.) 5 Sieverts

d.) 100 Sieverts

41. O-ethyl S-diisopropylaminomethyl methylphosphonothiolate is chemical name of following Poison:

a.) Botulinum Toxin

b.) VX

c.) Maitotoxin

d.) Polonium

42. VX was discovered by:

a.) Gerhard Schrader

b.) Paracelsus

c.) Ranaji Ghosh

d.) a & c

43. Lethal dose of Batrachotoxin (BTX) is:

a.) 10g/kg

b.) 0.2g/kg

c.) 3g/kg

d.) 1g/kg

44. Batrachotoxin (BTX) is produced by:

a.) Chemical synthesis

b.) By certain species of frogs

c.) Bacteria

d.) Plant

45. Maitotoxin is produced by:

a.) Gambierdiscus Toxicus

b.) Parachlorella Kessleri

c.) Mytilus galloprovincialis

d.) Ruditapes Philippinarum

46. Lethal dose of Maitotoxin is:

a.) 1g/kg

b.) 0.2g/kg

c.) 3g/kg

d.) 50ng/kg

47. Powder form of Cyanide is known as:

a.) Hydrogen Cyanide

b.) Potassium Cyanide

c.) Hydrocyanic Acid

d.) None

48. In which one of the following of the organ toxically significant level of cyanide may be found even after advanced decomposition of Body?

a.) Lever

b.) Spleen

c.) Heart

d.) Kidney

49. Who first of all described the association between chemical exposure and cancer?

a.) Percivall Pott

b.) Paracelsus

c.) Mathieu Orfila

d.) Ambroise Pare

50. Poisoning from Acetaminophen/Paracetamol can cause damage to:

a.) Bones

b.) Heart

c.) Lungs

d.) Liver

51. Some Poisons Impart characteristic colorations in body which is known as:

a.) Body color

b.) Postmortem Changes

c.) Postmortem Lividity

d.) Ante-mortem

52. Brick red color of post mortem lividity is seen in poisoning due to:

a.) Lead

b.) Arsenic

c.) Cyanide

d.) Carbon Monoxide

53. Cherry pink color of post mortem lividity is seen in poisoning due to:

a.) Carbon Monoxide

b.) Hydrogen Sulphide

c.) Lead

d.) Cyanide

54. Greenish Blue coolr of post mortem lividity is seen in poisoning due to:

a.) Lead

b.) Hydrogen Sulphide

c.) Cyanide

d.) Carbon Monoxide

55. Red (boiled Lobster) color of post mortem lividity is seen in poisoning due to:

a.) Lead

b.) Hydrogen Sulphide

c.) Boric Acid

d.) Carbon Monoxide

56. Brown color of post mortem lividity and garlic odor in stomach is seen in poisoning due to:

a.) Phosphorus

b.) Hydrogen Sulphide

c.) Cyanide

d.) Carbon Monoxide

57. Jaundice/Yellow color of post mortem lividity is seen in these poisonings, Except:

a.) Mushrooms

b.) Nitro Compounds

c.) Cyanide

d.) Picric Acid

58. Red-Brown color of post mortem lividity is seen in poisoning due to:

a.) Nitrites

b.) Silver Salts

c.) Cyanide

d.) Carbon Monoxide

59. Blue-Gray color of post mortem lividity is seen in poisoning due to:

a.) Phosphorus

b.) Silver Salts

c.) Cyanide

d.) Carbon Monoxide

60. Danbury tremor is seen in:

a.) Carbon Monoxide

b.) Lead poisoning

c.) Arsenic poisoning

d.) Mercury poisoning

61. Mad hatter is seen in:

a.) Carbon Monoxide

b.) Lead poisoning

c.) Arsenic poisoning

d.) Mercury poisoning

62. Acrodynia disease is caused by:

a.) Carbon Monoxide

b.) Mercury poisoning

c.) Lead poisoning

d.) Arsenic poisoning

63. How Danbury tremor begins and progress in body?

a.) It begins in the hand and progresses to lips, tongue, arms and legs.

b.) It begins in the head and progresses to lips, tongue, arms and legs.

c.) It begins from the face and progresses to lips, tongue, arms and legs.

d.) It begins in the legs and progresses to hips, Stomach, Chest and Head.

64. A toxic substance produced by biological system is referred as a _____:

a.) Xenobiotic

b.) Toxin

c.) Toxic

d.) Poison

65. Prolonged muscle relaxation after succinylcholine is an example of :

a.) Idiosyncratic Reaction

b.) Reaction related to a genetic increase in the activity of a liver enzyme

c.) IGE- mediated allergic reaction

d.) Immune complex reaction

66. Red colored hypostasis is seen in death because of following poison:

a.) Carbon Monoxide Poisoning

b.) Due to Cold

c.) Cyanide Poisoning

d.) Because of All

67. In case of acute carbon monoxide poisoning, coma and death with red color occurred at a carboxy haemoglobin level of:

a.)   30-40%

b.)   50-60%

c.)   60-70%

d.)   70-80%

68. Skin rash, confusion with lethargy, painful peripheral neuropathy and Alopecia are usually with lethargy are seen in poisoning with:

a.)   Thallium

b.) Arsenic

c.) Mercury

d.) Nickel

69. A person found on railway platform. He was talking irrelevant. He was having dry mouth with hot skin, dilated pupils, staggering gait and slurred speech. The most probable diagnosis is:

a.) Alcohol intoxication

b.) Carbamates poisoning

c.) Organophosphorous poisoning

d.) Dhatura poisoning

70. Coma cocktail Consist of Following, except:

a.) Naloxene

b.) Thiamine

c.) Pyridoxine

d.) Flumazenil

71. Which one of the arsenic compounds causes hemolysis?

a.) Arsenic Trioxide (As_2O_3)

b.) Arsenic Pentaoxide (As_2O_5)

c.) Arsine (AsH_3)

d.) All of the Above

72. Antidote for Arsenic Poisoning:

a.) Dimercaprol

b.) EDTA

c.) Penicillamine

d.) Sodium Nitrate

73. In Chronic Poisoning red pigmentation on skin occurs due to:

a.) Mercury

b.) Antimony

c.) Arsenic

d.) Lead

74. Bloody Rice Water Diarrhea occurs in Poisoning from:

a.) Mercury

b.) Antimony

c.) Arsenic

d.) Lead

75. Marsh Test is used for detection of

a.) Arsenic

b.) Copper

c.) Nitric Acid

d.) CO

76. Freshly precipitated iron oxide can neutralizes:

a.) Oxalic acid

b.) Alkalis

c.) Arsenic

d.) Acids

77. Delayed rigor mortis occurs in case of:

a.) Carbon Monoxide

b.) Lead

c.) Arsenic

d.) Copper

78. Poison which can be detected from burnt bone:

a.) Arsenic

b.) Mercury

c.) Chromium

d.) Lead

79. A Yellow stain on the paper in Gutzeit Test indicates the presence of:

a.) Mercury Poisoning

b.) Antimony Poisoning

c.) Arsenic Poisoning

d.) Lead Poisoning

80. Gutzeit Method is used for the extraction of:

a.) Inorganic Poison

b.) Volatile Inorganic Poison

c.) Volatile Organic Poison

d.) Gaseous Poison

81. Arsenic can be detected in presence of Antimony by which test?

a.) Reinsch Test

b.) Ammonium Molybdate Test

c.) Marsh's Test

d.) Gutzeit Test

82. All of these would show accumulation of arsenic in case of acute arsenic poisoning, except-

a.) Liver

b.) Bone marrow

c.) Skin

d.) Brain

83. Mee's lines are characteristics of-

a.) Mercury poisoning

b.) Barbiturate poisoning

c.) Arsenic Poisoning

d.) Dhatura Poisoning

84. **Fatty Yellow Liver is seen in poisoning with:**

a.) Arsenic

b.) Alcohol

c.) Mercury

d.) Organophosphorus

85. **Golden hair is seen in:**

a.) Carbon monoxide poisoning

b.) Phosphorus poisoning

c.) Barbiturates poisoning

d.) Arsenic Poisoning

86. **Which one of the following is used to preserve animal tissue, strengthen wood, carpet and other materials, but long exposure can lead to Leukemia and other varieties of cancer, ingesting a small amount of liquid can cause death.**

a.) Acetaldehyde

b.) Formaldehyde and Formic Acid

c.) Pyridine

d.) Acetic acid

87. In methyl alcohol poisoning, there is central nervous system depression, cardiac depression and optic nerve atrophy. These effects are produced due to:

a.) Formaldehyde and Formic Acid

b.) Acetaldehyde

c.) Pyridine

d.) Acetic acid

88. The average rate of alcohol elimination in breath per hour is:

a.) 3 µg/dl

b.) 6 µg/dl

c.) 15 µg/dl

d.) 30 µg/dl

89. Pyknometer method is used to estimate which of the following property of alcoholic beverage?

a.) Methanol content

b.) Ethyl alcohol content

c.) Volatile poison content

d.) Alcohol Content

90. Which one of the following is used to produce Toddy?

a.) Rice

b.) Wheat

c.) Mahua

d.) Palm

91. A toxicant produced by an animal is called

a.) Animal Toxin

b.) poison

c.) Venom

d.) Mycotoxin

92. Sodium Azide (Na_2N^3) has a mechanism of toxicity similar to:

a.) Cyanide

b.) Carbon Monoxide

c.) THC

d.) Benzene

93. Sodium Azide (Na_2N^3) is used in

a.) Refrigeration

b.) Air cooling

c.) Painting

d.) Air bags of car

94. Organs of dead body have an odor of bitter almond. Which volatile is poison?

a.) Phenol

b.) Chloroform

c.) Hydrocyanic acid

d.) Acetone

95. What volatile poison can be suspected as the reason of the poisoning in which Urine has a dark green color?

a.) Phenol

b.) Acetone

c.) Ethanol

d.) Methanol

96. The urine is turned olive or black olive due to poisoning by:

a.) Copper sulphate

b.) Isoamyl alcohol

c.) Phenol

d.) Iodoform

97. The color of stomach contents will turn black due to this poison:

a.) Oxalic Acid

b.) Isoamyl alcohol

c.) Phenol

d.) Iodoform

98. Which one of the following poisoning may cause pink color stomach wall:

a.) Nitric Acid

b.) Copper sulphate

c.) Soneryl

d.) Amytal

99. The color of stomach contents will turn bluish green due to this poison:

a.) Oxalic Acid

b.) Copper Sulphate

c.) Phenol

d.) Iodoform

100. The color of stomach contents will turn Slate due to this poison:

a.) Oxalic Acid

b.) Copper Sulphate

c.) Phenol

d.) Mercury

101. Administration by Oral gavage of a test compound that is highly metabolized by the liver vs subcutaneous injection will most likely result in:

a.)   More systemic toxicity

b.)   More local irritation at the site of administration caused by the compound

c.)   lower levels of metabolites in the systemic circulation

d.)   Less parent compound present in the systemic circulation

102. Which external sign indicates the phenol poisoning in Urine Sample?

a.)   Olive color

b.)   red color

c.)   Strong Odor of Urine

d.)   Yellow color

103. What method is used to isolate Chloral Hydrate poison?

a.)   Mineralization

b.)   Extraction method

c.)   Steam Distillation

d.)   Chromatographic method

104. The vessel for collection of the distillate of Cyanide poisoning by steam distillation method must contain:

a.)   Solution of Sodium Chloride

b.) Solution of Sodium Hydroxide

c.) Solution of Chloride Acid

d.) Solution of Iodine

105. 'Black foot' disease is caused by _____

a.) Chromium

b.) Mercury

c.) Arsenic

d.) Lead

106. A blackened Perforated nasal septum is an indication for addiction to:

a.) Alcohol

b.) Barbiturates

c.) Hashish

d.) Methamphetamine

107. Color that can be observed in nitric acid toxicity is

a.) Yellow

b.) Blue

c.) Green

d.) Red

108. Brown colored urine is seen in poisoning due to:

a.) Carbon Monoxide

b.) Nitric Acid

c.) Sulphur

d.) Arsenic

109. Cadmium is a highly toxic metal that causes:

a.) Damage to renal tubules

b.) GI tract irritation

c.) Cancer

d.) All

110. 'Itai-itai' disease is caused by_____

a.) Cadmium

b.) Mercury

c.) Lead

d.) Copper

111. What is the meaning of Itai Itai desease?

a.) Painful

b.) Ouch, Ouch

c.) Disease

d.) None

112. In Itai Itai disease which parts/Organ of body affected?

a.) Kidney and bones

b.) Heart and Lungs

c.) Whole body

d.) Hands and Legs

113. _____uses paralysis of respiratory muscles.

a.) Barbiturates

b.) Heroin

c.) Botulinum

d.) All of the above

114. A person with hot skin, dry mouth, talking irrelevant, dilated pupils, staggering gait and slurred speech. The most probable diagnosis is:

a.) Alcohol intoxication

b.) Organophosphorous poisoning

c.) Dhatura poisoning

d.) Carbamates poisoning

115. A chemical substance that affects the processes of the mind or body and used in the diagnosis, treatment, or prevention of a disease:

a.) Medicine

b.) Barbiturates

c.) Poison

d.) Drug

116. Any type of natural or synthetic matter/substance which can cause grave harm or death or any psychological disturbance if inhaled, ingested or absorbed via skin, is known as:

a.) Drug

b.) Poison

c.) P-DMAB

d.) Beverages

117. Paraquat Poisoning causes:

a.) Renal failure

b.) Cardiac failure

c.) Respiratory failure

d.) Multiple organ failure

118. Cyanosis is caused by:

a.) A Decreased concentration of Oxyhemoglobin

b.) A Decreased concentration of Hemoglobin

c.) An Increased concentration of reduced hemoglobin

d.) An Increased concentration of Oxyhemoglobin

119. Which of the following toxicity can occur due to single exposure?

a.) Acute toxicity

b.) Sub-chronic toxicity

c.) Chronic toxicity

d.) Sub-acute toxicity

120. Ecstasy toxicity causes:

a.) Hypereflexia

b.) Trismus

c.) Dilated pupils & Visual Hallucinations

d.) All of the above

121. A person has bought a bottle of liquor from local shop and consumes it and within 1 hour of consumption he start vomiting, he develops blurred vision and confusions. He has been brought to the hospital in emergency situation. He should be treated with:

a.) Diazepam

b.) Barbiturates

c.) Ethanol

d.) Ethyl alcohol

122. All of the following are treatment options for toxic alcohol poisoning, except:

a.) Fomepizole

b.) Hydroxycobalamin

c.) Thiamine

d.) Folic acid

123. Widmark's formula is used for estimation of:

a.) Cyanides

b.) Arsenic

c.) Benzene

d.) Blood Alcohol

124. McEwan's sign is seen in:

a.) Alcohol Intoxication

b.) Arsenic Poisoning

c.) Cyanide Poisoning

d.) Lead Poisoning

125. Fatal dose of Methyl Alcohol is:

a.) 10 ml

b.) 20 ml

c.) 60 to 120 ml

d.) 15 to 25 ml

126. **Hyperthermia in a patient of poisoning is a pointer to all, except:**

a.) Ecstasy

b.) Selective serotonin reuptake inhibitor

c.) Salicylates

d.) Chlorpromazine

127. **Bluish discoloration of neck of tooth due to:**

a.) Alcohol

b.) Arsenic

c.) Cyanide

d.) Nicotine

128. **Which one of the following color test's reagent is made up of Selenous acid?**

a.) Mecke's Test

b.) Marquis Test

c.) Von-Urk's Test

d.) Chen's Test

129. **The phrase that best defines "Toxicodynamics" is the:**

a.) Dynamic nature of toxic effects among various species

b.) Dose range between desired biological effects and adverse health effects c.) Linkage between Dose and Exposure

d.) Linkage between Response and Dose

130. Sodium fluoride is added as preservative in the following concentration for chemical analysis of blood and urine:

a.) 150 mg/10 ml

b.) 50 mg/10 ml

c.) 10 mg/10 ml

d.) 200 mg/10 ml

131. Preservative used for preservation of viscera in all cases of poisoning but not in the case of acid poisoning (except carbolic acid):

a.) Saturated solution of Sodium Chloride

b.) 10% Formalin

c.) Alcohol

d.) Acetone

132. Preservative used for preservation of viscera for Acid poisoning except Carbolic acid Poisoning:

a.) Saturated solution sodium chloride

b.) Rectified Spirit

c.) Alcohol

d.) 10% Formalin

133. Preservative used for preservation of viscera in case of Carbon Monoxide Poisoning:

a.) Saturated solution sodium chloride

b.) Rectified Spirit

c.) A layer of Paraffin (to prevent escape of gas)

d.) 10% Formalin

134. Following Gaseous Poison have different types of Odour, Except:

a.) Hydrogen sulphide

b.) Ammonia

c.) Phosphine

d.) Carbon monoxide

135. In _____ poisoning, the gas has greater affinity combines easily with haemoglobin and make them unable to carry oxygen to various tissues of the body.

a.) Arsenic

b.) Mercury

c.) Carbon-mono oxide

d.) Benzene

136. Carbon Monoxide is:

a.) Soluble in water

b.) Miscible with water

c.) Insoluble in water

d.) None

137. In Micro Diffusion Technique (Feld Stein) reduction of palladium chloride to grey or black is positive for:

a.) Carbon Monoxide

b.) Hydrogen Sulphide

c.) Phosphine

d.) Chlorine

138. What is the mode of action of carbon monoxide (CO)?

a.) It reduces the oxygen absorption by directly or indirectly damaging the alveoli.

b.) It destroys the red blood cells.

c.) Combines with hemoglobin to reduce oxygen carrying capacity of RBCs.

d.) It alters the structure of the hemoglobin.

139. Preservative used for preservation of blood in case of Poisoning;

a.) Potassium Oxalate and Sodium fluoride

b.) 50% Formalin

c.) Alcohol

d.) Rectified Spirit

140. CSF is required to be preserved in :

a.) Alcohol Poisoning

b.) Arsenic Poisoning

c.) Carbon monoxide poisoning

d.) Copper Poisoning

141. Preservative used in urine sample for chemical analysis is:

a.) Formalin

b.) EDTA

c.) Alcohol

d.) Thymol

142. Elapidaes are:

a.) Vasculotoxic

b.) Neurotoxic

c.) Musculotoxic

d.) Nontoxic

143. Magnan's symptoms are characteristic symptoms of following poisoning:

a.) Alcohol

b.) Charas

c.) Cocaine

d.) Ecstasy

144. This poison can lead to sex perversion?

a.) Alcohol

b.) Charas

c.) Cocaine

d.) Ecstasy

145. Common toxicity target of inorganic mercuric salts and organic mercury is:

a.) Heart

b.) Liver

c.) Kidney

d.) Lungs

146. Using Ferric Chloride test in salicylate toxicity turns urine to:

a.) Pink color

b.) Purple Color

c.) Black color

d.) Red Purple

147. Burning sensation after exposure to chilli pepper is an example of:

a.) Sensitization

b.) Dermatitis

c.) Chemesthesis

d.) Receptor Activation

148. Which of the following toxins comes from the castor beans?

a.) Ricin

b.) THC

c.) Pesticides

d.) Strychnine

149. Fatal dose of Castor bean is:

a.) 2mg for a man weighing 60kg

b.) 6mg for a man weighing 60kg

c.) 60mg for a man weighing 60kg

d.) 30mg for a man weighing 60kg

150. Ricin was first used in to kill:

a.) Boris Korczak,1981

b.) James Dalton Bell,1997

c.) Georgi Markov,1978

d.) Shannon Richardson,2013

151. Which part of the castor plant is poisonous?

a.) Leaf

b.) Root

c.) Seeds

d.) Overall Plant

152. Hunan hand syndrome is produced by following:

a.) Chili Seed

b.) Castor Seed

c.) Croton Seed

d.) Marking Nut

153. One vial of 10 ml Antivenom serum can neutralize:

a.) 6 mg of Russell's viper venom

b.) 6 mg of Cobra venom

c.) 4.5 mg of common krait venom

d.) 4.5 mg of saw scaled viper venom

e.) All of the above

154. Following term is refers to the capsule of papaver somniferum after opium has been extracted from it:

a.) Poppy Seeds

b.) Opium Extracts

c.) Post Ka Doda

d.) Extracted Poppy

155. Derivatives of Opium is:

a.) Morphine

b.) Codeine

c.) Heroine

d.) All

156. After smoking of the opium the left out residue is known as:

a.) Opium leftover

b.) Opium extracts

c.) Dross Opium

d.) Deodrized Opium

157. Deodrized opium is prepared by treating opium with which of the following?

a.) Chlorofrom

b.) Methyl Alcohol

c.) Petroleum Ether

d.) Acetone

158. The source of most analgesics narcotic is:

a.) White Oliver

b.) Marijuana

c.) Dahlia

d.) Opium

159. Scientific name of Opium is:

a.) Papaver Sominiferum

b.) Cannabis Sativa

c.) Papa Sominiferus

d.) Marijuana

160. The range of Papaverine in Opium is:

a.) 10-20%

b.) 0-0.5%

c.) 0.5-1.3%

d.) 0.2-1%

161. Which of the following substance of opium is used in Cough Syrups?

a.) Morphine

b.) Codeine

c.) Thebaine

d.) Papaverine

162. All Parts of Opium poppy is known as:

a.) Poppy Straw

b.) Poppin

c.) Poppy

d.) Cannabis

163. Wilson's disease is associated with the accumulation of following metal-

a.) Thalium

b.) Copper

c.) Arsenic

d.) Zinc

164. Restriction enzymes are used in one of these techniques:

a.) Polymerization

b.) Sequencing

c.) Genotyping

d.) RFLP

165. Which of the following is commonly known as ecstasy?

a.) Methamphetamine

b.) Amphetamine

c.) methylenedioxymethamphetamine

d.) 3,4-methylenedioxymethamphetamine (MDMA).

166. Electrophoresis is mainly used for:

a.) Separates the molecules

b.) For DNA Extraction

c.) Differentiate the biological sample

d.) Separate the Electric Current

167. In the case of heavy metal or arsenic compound poisoning the following antidote is used:

a.) Methyl blue

b.) Vitamin B12

c.) Unithiol

d.) Glucagon

168. Antidote for Copper Poisoning:

a.) Penicillamine

b.) Dimercaprol

c.) EDTA

d.) a & b

Forensic Toxicology

169. Calcium EDTA is use as Antidote for following metal poisoning:

a.) Mercury

b.) Antimony

c.) Arsenic

d.) Lead

170. The best antidote to be given in cases of ethylene glycol toxicities is:

a.) Ethanol

b.) Fomepizole

c.) Methanol

d.) Aniline

171. Antidote for acetaminophen/Paracetomol:

a.) Sodium Nitrate

b.) EDTA

c.) Dimercaprol

d.) N-acetylcysteine

172. Milk of Magnesia or soap solution can be used in poisoning due to:

a.) Alkali

b.) Acids

c.) Metal

d.) Alkaloids

173. Chemical name of Milk of magnesia is:

a.) Magnesium Hydroxide

b.) Magnesium oxide

c.) Magnesium sulphate

d.) Magnesium carbonate

174. Parlidoxime is used in the treatment of this poison:

a.) Phosphorus

b.) Pyrethrins

c.) Parathion

d.) Endrin

175. In alkali poisoning _____ can be used.

a.) Milk

b.) Luke Warm Water

c.) Tinned Juice or Vinegar

d.) Lime

176. What specific antidote is used for Cyanide Poisoning?

a.) EDTA

b.) Sodium Nitrate

c.) Fuller's Earth

d.) Penicillamine

177. At barium salt poisoning such specific chemical antidote is used:

a.) Potassium iodide

b.) Sodium chloride

c.) Sodium sulphate

d.) Sodium carbonate

178. What specific antidote is used for poisoning by iron?

a.) Deferoxamine

b.) Bemegride

c.) Penicillamine

d.) Protamine sulphate

179. What specific antidote is used for Organophosphate Poisoning?

a.) Deferoxamine

b.) Bemegride

c.) Penicillamine

d.) Atropine

180. Ethanol is used as an antidote in methanol poisoning because

a.) Ethanol competes for choline esterase enzyme

b.) Ethanol competes for choline ADH enzyme

c.) Ethanol by product is formic acid

d.) Ethanol is cheap and easily available

181. Which of the following is not the metabolite of ethanol?

a.) Methanol

b.) Ethanol

c.) Acetic Acid

d.) Acetone

182. MAcEwen's sign is a manifestation of massive intake of:

a.) Ethanol

b.) Arsenic

c.) Opium

d.) Methyl Alcohol

183. One of the following symptom is an indication of severe ethanol intoxication:

a.) Euphoria

b.) Furious behavior

c.) Muscular incoordination

d.) All of the above

184. Blindness can be caused by the following:

a.) Methanol

b.) Ethyl Alcohol

c.) Arsenic

d.) Morphine

185. Following comment is true regarding methanol toxicity.

a.) Methanol causes direct toxicity to optical nerves after absorption.

b.) Methanol is less toxic than ethanol.

c.) Aldehyde dehydrogenase converts methanol into formaldehyde which causes blindness.

d.) Alcohol dehydrogenase and aldehyde dehydrogenase converts methanol into formic acid which causes blindness.

186. At the time of isolating Methanol in steam distillation method for volatile poisons, methanol is collected in:

a) Empty Vessel

b) Vessel with Sodium Hydroxide

c) Vessel with Hydrochloric Acid

d) Cooled Vessel

187. Magnesium Oxide

a.) Neutralizes acids

b.) Absorb Acids

c.) Precipitate Acids

d.) Make Acid

188. The reference dose (RfD) is generally determined by applying which of the following default procedures?

a.) An uncertainty factor of 100 is applied to the NOAEL in chronic animal studies

b.) a risk factor of 1000 is applied to the NOAEL in chronic animal studies

c.) an uncertainty factor between 10,000 and 1 million is applied to the NOEL from chronic animal studies

d.) a risk factor of 10,000 is applied to the NOAEL in subchronic animal studies

189. The most common target organ of toxicity is the:

a.) Stomach

b.) Eyes

c.) Central Nervous System

d.) Lungs

190. Less affected Organs in human from toxicity:

a.) Muscle And Bone

b.) Hematopoietc system and lungs

c.) Brain And Peripheral Nerves

d.) Liver And Kidney

191. "*Ames Test*" is used to detect:

a.) Hepatotoxic potential of chemicals in cell cultures

b.) Salmonella typhimurium infection

c.) Mutagenic potential of chemicals using in vitro test with mutant strains of Salnonella typhimurium

d.) Solamonella typhi infection

192. Mineralization of the biological samples when heating in the crucible to high temperature at free air is named:

a.) Extraction

b.) Dry Ashing

c.) Distillation

d.) Wet Ashing

193. Which scientist was the first to suggest the idea of the necessity of the mineralization in the study of the biological material for the presence of heavy metal compounds:

a.) Ravdanikis P. K

b.) Krilova A. N.

c.) Nelyubin A. P

d.) Zaykovskiy F. V.

194. Which one of the following metallic poison is isolated from the biological matter with the help of mineralization destruction?

a.) Silver

b.) Thallium

c.) Cadmium

d.) Mercury

195. For the prevention of mercury loss during forensic-toxicological study of the biological material some special isolation method is used. This method is named:

a.) Destruction

b.) Disintegration

c.) Mineralization

d.) Denaturation

196. What method is used for isolation of mercury compounds from the biological material?

a.) Mineralization

b.) Destruction

c.) Steam distillation

d.) Extraction with acidified ethanol

197. **A drug that induces Changes in perception and mood without affecting brain activity is known as:**

a.) Stimulant

b.) Hallucinogen

c.) Dizziness

d.) Mood Swing

198. _____ is the process of removing nitric, nitrogenous, nitrososulphuric acids and nitrogen oxides from the mineralizate.

a.) Denitration

b.) Mineralization

c.) Denaturation

d.) Destruction

199. **What method of the denitration is the most widespread and fast?**

a.) Distillation

b.) By urea

c.) By formalin

d.) Hydrolysis

200. **What reagent is used for denitration?**

a.) Sodium sulphite

b.) Urea

c.) Sodium of thiosulphate

d.) Solution of formaldehyde

201. Which scientist suggested the method of the mineralizate denitration using formaldehyde?

a.) Krylova A. N.

b.) Zaykovskiy F. V.

c.) Kramarenko V. F

d.) Shvaykova M. D

202. Whit precipitate was obtained in the process of metallic poison isolation from the biological material. The mineralization was carried out by the mixture of H_2SO_4 and HNO_3. Following poison can be presence:

a.) Lead

b.) Thallium

c.) Copper

d.) Zinc

203. What metallic poison is detected with KI by the reaction of "gold rain formation"?

a.) Cu^{2+}

b.) Pb^{2+}

c.) Ag^+

d.) Ba2+

204. Amenorrhoea and infertility are the possible complications of chronic poisoning with:

a.) Mercury

b.) Lead

c.) Zinc

d.) Chromium

205. Ciguatera toxin is produced by:

a.) Jelly Fish

b.) Star Fish

c.) Shark

d.) Barracuda Fish

206. Malformation of Tooth Enamel is caused by:

a.) Fluoride

b.) CO

c.) Iron

d.) Lithium

207. When studying the mineralizate for the presence of barium cations the reaction with sodium rhodizonate is used which produce this color:

a.) Black

b.) Purple

c.) Red

d.) Yellow

208. _____ is also known as "Thorn Apple"?

a.) Dhatura Stramonium

b.) Hashish

c.) Dhatura

d.) Mushrooms

209. **Ganja is Obtained From which part of Cannabis Plant:**

a.) Leaves

b.) Twigs

c.) Flowering Tops

d.) Roots

210. **Hashish is Produced from:**

a.) Leaves of Cannabis Indica

b.) Roots of Cannabis Indica

c.) Resin Exudate of Cannabis Indica

d.) Twigs of Cannabis Indica

211. _____ also used as an "Arrow Poison" :

a.) Nux Vomica

b.) Hashish

c.) Cocaine

d.) Arsenic

212. The cannabis plant secretes a sticky resin known as:

a.) Nux Vomica

b.) Hashish

c.) Cocaine

d.) Arsenic

213. _____ known as Sweet Poison:

a.) Cyanide

b.) Aconite

c.) Phosphine

d.) Methanol

214. Which type of Phosphorus highly Toxic?

a.) Yellow Phosphorus

b.) Red Phosphorus

c.) Black Phosphorus

d.) Green Phosphorus

215. Yellow phosphorus oxidises with formation of pale yellow fumes glowing around after exposure to air. This phenomenon is known as:

a.) Glowing of phosphorus

b.) Phosphorus oxidation

c.) Phosphorescence

d.) Yellow glow

216. Which type of Phosphorus is Non-Toxic?

a.) Yellow Phosphorus

b.) Red Phosphorus

c.) Black Phosphorus

d.) Green Phosphorus

217. Which substance is used in sides of match box?

a.) Yellow Phosphorus

b.) Sulphur

c.) Red Phosphorus

d.) Potassium Chlorate

218. Phosphorus will spontaneously ignite if exposed to air in 30⁰C, that's why it kept in following solution:

a.) Formaldehyde

b.) Water

c.) Kerosene oil

d.) b & c

219. When you strike and burn a match, it releases _____:

a.) Carbon dioxide

b.) Carbon monoxide

c.) Methane

d.) Sulphur dioxide

220. Surma (Collyrium for the eyes) is :

a.) Tetra-ethyl Lead

b.) Lead acetate

c.) Lead Oxide

d.) Lead Sulphide

221. Red Lead or Vermillion is:

a.) Lead Acetate

b.) Lead Carbonate

c.) Lead Tetraoxide

d.) Lead Oxide

222. Least Toxic Form of Lead is:

a.) Tetra-ethyl Lead

b.) Lead acetate

c.) Lead Oxide

d.) Lead Sulphide

223. Sideroblastic anemia is seen in poisoning with

a.) Mercury

b.) Lead

c.) Arsenic

d.) Cyanide

224. All are features of Lead Poisoning, except:

a.) Abdominal Pain

b.) Nephropathy

c.) Diarrhea

d.) Encephalopathy

225. Burton's line seen in Poisoning with?

a.) Yellow Phosphorus

b.) Lead

c.) Sulphur

d.) Potassium Chlorate

226. Average fatal period of Lead poisoning is :

a.) 2-4 hours

b.) 10-15 hours

c.) In few minutes

d.) 1-2 days

227. Toxicity of lead depends on which factor?

a.) Solubility

b.) Exposure

c.) Insolubility

d.) All of the above

228. _____ is the earliest sign of lead poisoning.

a.) Concussion mercurialis

b.) Eczema

c.) Mees lines

d.) Punctate Basophilia

229. Mercury is the only metal that is _____ in room temperature.

a.) Solid

b.) Liquid

c.) Semi-Solid

d.) Vapor

230. Fatal dose of Thallium:

a.) About 1gm

b.) About 1.5gm

c.) About 2-3gm

d.) About 4gm

231. Croton Tiglium is:

a.) Arandi

b.) Jamal gota

c.) Gunchi

d.) Chillies

232. The active principle of Croton Tiglium is:

a.) Ricin

b.) Abrin

c.) Crotin

d.) None

233. Arrange the following in the increasing order of their active principle:

a.) Charas, Bhang, Hashish oil, ganja

b.) Bhang, ganja, Charas, Hashish oil

c.) Bhang, Hashish oil, Charas, ganja

d.) Charas, Hashish oil, ganja, Bhang

234. In case of drug abuse during pregnancy following specimens would be suitable:

a.) Meconium

b.) Hair

c.) Urine

d.) a & b

235. Adverse reaction to drugs prescribed by Doctor is known as:

a.) Corrosive poisoning

b.) Idiosyncrasy

c.) Iatrogenic Poisoning

d.) Poisoning

236. BAL full Form:

a.) Bi-Anti Liquid

b.) British Anti-Lewisite

c.) British Anti-Liquid

d.) British Acute-Liquid

237. BAL is a common name of :

a.) Dimercaprol (2,3-dimercaptopropanol)

b.) Dimercaprol (1,2-dimercaptopropanol)

c.) Dimercaprol (1-dimercaptopropanol)

d.) Diimercaprol (dimercaptopropanol)

238. BAL is effective against the effect of:

a.) Phosphide poisoning

b.) Heavy Metal Poisoning

c.) Lead Poisoning

d.) Arsenic Poisoning

239. BAL is antidote for the following metal poisons, but used to treat with EDTA for the following one:

a.) Mercury

b.) Antimony

c.) Arsenic

d.) Lead

240. Which Vitamin is also a Hormone?

a.) Vitamin C

b.) Vitamin D

c.) Vitamin B_{12}

d.) Vitamin A

241. Poisoning From Carbolic Acid is known as:

a.) Carbolic poisoning

b.) Carbo Poison

c.) Carbolism

d.) Carbolic

242. In case of Carbolic Acid poisoning urine color turned olive green, this state is known as:

a.) Carbolic poisoning

b.) Carboluria

c.) Carbolism

d.) Carbolist

243. Which oil is used for stomach wash in carbolic acid poisoning?

a.) Olive oil

b.) Castor oil

c.) Mustard oil

d.) a & b

244. Phossy jaw is seen in which poisoning?

a.) Red Phosphorus

b.) Yellow Phosphorus

c.) Arsenic

d.) Carbamate

245. It is not Poisonous if taken by mouth:

a.) Arsenic

b.) Mercury

c.) Lead

d.) Thallium

246. Fatal dose of Mercuric Chloride:

a.) 0.5-1gm

b.) 1-2gm

c.) 5-10gm

d.) 2-3gm

247. Which of the following chelating agents is recommended for acute Lead Poisoning with signs of encephalopathy?

a.) Dimercaprol

b.) Calcium EDTA

c.) Dimercaprol+Calcium EDTA

d.) Succimer

248. All of the following symptoms can occur with Ciguatera poisoning, except:

a.) Metallic taste

b.) Flushing

c.) Myalgias

d.) Painful teeth

249. All of the following are treatment options for toxic alcohol poisoning, except:

a.) Fomepizole

b.) Thiamine

c.) Hydroxocobalamin

d.) Folic Acid

250. Ecotoxicology is the study of:

a.) Chemical Interaction of organism and environment

b.) Chemical Interaction of organism and animal

c.) Physical Interaction of Organism and environment

d.) Physical Interaction of organisms

251. Acute aquatic toxicity is measured in :

a.) EC

b.) ES

c.) AC

d.) AS

252. Which species is used as screening of chemicals:

a.) Starfish

b.) Zebrafish

c.) Eisinia Foetida

d.) Cat fish

253. Melamine can cause kidney stones by forming hydrogen bonds with:

a.) Uric Acid

b.) Cyanuric Acid

c.) a & b

d.) Nitric Acid

254. The interaction of melamine and cyanuric acid to cause renal toxicity is an example of:

a.) Poisoning

b.) Synergism

c.) Antagonism

d.) Potentization

255. Which category of insecticidal compounds presents a problem of persistent residues in fatty tissues of animals:

a.) Organochlorines

b.) Organophosphorus

c.) Organophosphates

d.) Carbamates

256. Which is not Anion?

a.) Halides

b.) Chlorate

c.) Nitrite

d.) Copper

257. Tear gas is also known as

a.) Chloroacetophenon

b.) Methylisocyanide

c.) Hydrogensulphide

d.) Chlorine

258. Which is not a Pesticide?

a.) Organophosphorous

b.) Organochloro

c.) Carbamates

d.) Sulphurdioxide

259. DDT full form is:

a.) Dichloro Diphenyl Trichloroethane

b.) Dichlorine Diphenolic Trichloro

c.) Di Diphenolic Trichloroethane

d.) Dichlo Diphenol Triethane

260. DDT is a:

a.) Organophosphorus Insecticides

b.) Organochloro Pesticides

c.) Carbamate Pesticides

d.) Organophosphrous Pesticides

261. What happens to DDT when it enters the body?

a.) It is water soluble and easily excreted out from the body.

b.) It is converted into an active metabolite.

c.) It bypasses the metabolism and excreted as such

d.) It is fat soluble and stored in fat tissue.

262. These are example of Synergism, except:

a.) Alcohol & Barbiturates

b.) Pyrethrins & Pyrethroid

c.) Carbon Tetra Chloride & Ethanol

d.) Codeine And Cannabis

263. Symptoms of Poisoning, except:

a.) Vomiting

b.) Diarrhoea

c.) Coma

d.) Chattering

264. Poisons commonly involved when symptom is Jaundice:

a.) Carbon monoxide

b.) Hepatotoxic

c.) Arsenic

d.) Cyanide

265. Hepatotoxic poisons are:

a.) Arsenic

b.) Carbon Tetrachloride

c.) Vinyl Chloride

d.) Flucoxacillin

e.) All of the above

266. Human body shows symptom of Flushed Pink skin after being affected by these poisons, Except:

a.) Alcohol

b.) Cocaine

c.) Cyanide

d.) Carbon Monoxide

267. Red venous blood suggest poisoning from:

a.) Cyanide

b.) Alcohol

c.) Barbiturates

d.) Methaemoglobinaemia

268. Brown Arterial blood may suggest poisoning from:

a.) Cyanide

b.) Alcohol

c.) Barbiturates

d.) Methaemoglobinaemia

269. Urine may be cloudy or red or brown due to :

a.) Haematuria

b.) Haemoglobinuria

c.) Myoglobinuria

d.) All

270. Emetics are the Substance, which produce_____:

a.) Vomiting

b.) Sweating

c.) Diarrhea

d.) Pupil Dilation

271. Emesis should be avoided in_____:

a.) Corrosive Poisoning

b.) Ingestion of Petroleum distillates

c.) Coma

d.) All

272. Emetics are contraindicated in poisoning of:

a.) Arsenic

b.) Cyanide

c.) Kerosene

d.) Organophosphorus

273. Who are Arsenophagist?

a.) Who use Arsenic for laboratory purpose

b.) Who use Arsenic in criminal activities

c.) Who can tolerate Arsenic in high Doses

d.) All of the above

274. Household emetics are:

a.) Lukewarm water

b.) Water with Salt

c.) 15gm mustard powder in 200 ml of water

d.) All of the Above

275. Method of emptying stomach of an unconscious patient is:

a.) Luke warm water

b.) Gastric Aspiration and Lavage

c.) Zinc sulphate(1-2gm) in water(200ml)

d.) Apomorphine

276. Demulcents should not be given in case of:

a.) Phosphorus Poisoning

b.) Strychinine Poisoning

c.) Acid nitric

d.) Alkalies

277. Bulky food like banana acts as a mechanical antidote for:

a.) Arsenic

b.) Barbiturates

c.) Phosphorous

d.) Glass

278. Strong concentrated alkalies are not used as antidote, because:

a.) Production of big amount of CO_2

b.) Production of toxic gases

c.) Reducing the CO_2 amount

d.) Decreasing the level of CO_2

279. Dilute Acetic Acid Neutralizes

a.) Acid

b.) Alkalis

c.) Phosphorus

d.) Lead

280. Acids Neutralizes by

a.) Magnesium oxide or Calcium oxide

b.) Lime

c.) Copper sulphate

d.) Tannin

281. Drug interact with their receptors sites by forming

a.) Ionic bond

b.) Hydrogen bond

c.) Vander walls bond

d.) All of the above

282. EDTA Full Form:

a.) Ethylene Diamine Tetra Acetate

b.) Ethyl Di Tetra Acetate

c.) Ethylene Dioxy Tertiary Acetate

d.) Ethyl Diamine Tetra Acid

283. Benzodiazepines are least effective in:

a.) Alcohol withdrawal syndrome

b.) Obsessive-Compulsive Disorder

c.) Phobias

d.) All of the above

284. Benzodiazepines act on the CNS through the following mechanism:

a.) Increasing the activity of GABA

b.) Decreasing the activity of GABA

c.) Pausing the activity of GABA

d.) All of the above

285. Any material substance in the universe wherein the active constituents may be dispersed, accumulated, left, absorbed or chemically bound is known as:

a.) Quantitation

b.) Matrix

c.) Toxic

d.) None of above

286. Its involves separation of a crystalloid from a colloid by filtering through a semi-permeable membrane:

a.) Dialysis

b.) Sublimation

c.) Partition

d.) Absorption

287. _____ is applicable to isolate a toxicant in solid matrices.

a.) Dialysis

b.) Sublimation

c.) Absorption

d.) Partition

288. The extraction of metals in biological matrices may be carried out by the following methods:

a.) Dry Ashing Method

b.) Wet Digestion or Acid Digestion Method

c.) Fresenius and Babo Method

d.) All of the above

289. Opium poisoning is treated with:

a.) Naloxone

b.) Atropine

c.) Neostigmine

d.) Physostigmine

290. CAGA questionnaire is a widely used screening test for:

a.) Alcohol Problem

b.) Opium Poisoning

c.) Barbiturate Poisoning

d.) Heavy Metal Poisoning

291. Which method is suitable for mercury:

a.) Dry Ashing Method

b.) Fresenium and Babo Method

c.) Wet Digestion Method

d.) Selective Chemical Treatment

292. Erethism occours in:

a.) Mercury

b.) Lead

c.) Copper

d.) Arsenic

293. Lead encephalopathy is most commonly seen in:

a.) Pregnant woman

b.) Old person

c.) Children

d.) Painters

294. Which method is used to extract Toxic Anions from Forensic Matrices?

a.) Protein Precipitation

b.) Dialysis

c.) Micro diffusion

d.) All of the above

295. This method is useful for preliminary analysis of alkaloids, tranquilizing drugs and barbiturate etc.:

a.) Ammonium Sulphate Method

b.) Stas-otto method

c.) Selective Chemical Method

d.) Wet Digestion Method

296. Which Volatile Poison is not Miscible with Water?

a.) Acetaldehyde

b.) Acetone

c.) Isopropyl Alcohol

d.) Benzene

297. Which Volatile Poison is Slightly Soluble in Water?

a.) Aniline

b.) Carbon di-sulphide

c.) Chloroform

d.) Naphthalene

298. The substance used by athletes for doping is:

a.) Marijuana

b.) Barbituric Acid

c.) Nandrolone

d.) Lysergic Acid

299. A practice, in which poisons use to ingest to build immunity against toxic substance is known as:

a.) Antibiotic

b.) Mithridatism

c.) Antitoxic

d.) Tolerance

300. Which Volatile Poison has a Burning Taste?

a.) Formaldehyde

b.) Arsine

c.) Ethyl Alcohol

d.) Isopropyl Alcohol

301. Boiling range of Kerosene is:

a.) 98-100°C

b.) 150-300°C

c.) 300-400°C

d.) 50-100°C

302. Domestic kerosene is blue, due to:

a.) Anthracene

b.) Coomassie Brilliant Blue

c.) Anthraquinone

d.) Eosine

303. Which volatile poison is oil?

a.) Kerosene

b.) Nitrobenzene

c.) Turpentine

d.) All of the above

304. A child aged about 11 year ingested a clear liquid, he vomited twice, had cough with tachypnea. After 24 hours

bronchopneumonia also developed. These symptoms can be of following poisoning:

a.) Ethanol

b.) Methanol

c.) Kerosene oil

d.) Phenol

305. Characteristic Hexagonal crystals of iodoform are seen in Iodoform test indicates the presence of:

a.) Acetone

b.) Acetaldehyde

c.) Pyridine

d.) Carbondisulphide

306. Formation of Purple color in Schiff's reagent test confirms the presence of:

a.) Acetone

b.) Methanol

c.) Formaldehyde

d.) Ethyl Alcohol

307. Formation of deep blue in Sulphomolybdic Acid indicates the presence of:

a.) Acetone

b.) Acetaldehyde

c.) Formaldehyde

d.) Ethyl Alcohol

308. Schiff's reagent Test for Methanol produce:

a.) Blue color

b.) Pink Color

c.) Purple color

d.) Black Color

309. Violet color observed in Chromotropic Acid Test, this can be present:

a.) Methanol

b.) Ethanol

c.) Ethyl Alcohol

d.) Isopropyl Alcohol

310. Fujiwara Test is Preliminary Test For:

a.) Arsenic

b.) Mercury

c.) Phosphorus

d.) Chloroform

311. **Fujiwara Test produces which color for confirmation of Chloroform?**

a.) Brown to black color

b.) Pink to Red Color

c.) Brown to Yellow Color

d.) White Precipitate

312. **The Scott Test is a Preliminary Colorimetric Method to analyze:**

a.) Heroin

b.) Cocaine

c.) Barbiturates

d.) Opium

313. **Prussian Blue Test indicates the presence of:**

a.) Ethanol

b.) Kerosene

c.) Hydrocyanic Acid

d.) Turpentine

314. **Pink color observed in Cobalt Thio-Cyanate Test, Following Compound Present:**

a.) Heroin

b.) Caffeine

c.) Cocaine

d.) Diazepam

315. Yellow crystals forms in Picric Acid test indicates the presence of:

a.) Nicotine

b.) Nitrobenzene

c.) Hydrocyanic Acid

d.) Naphthalene

316. Roussin's Test produced crystalline ruby red needle shape crystals indicates the presence of:

a.) Nicotine

b.) Naphthalene

c.) Ethylene

d.) Phenyl

317. Vitalis Test performed for detection of:

a.) Dhatura

b.) Arsenic

c.) Morphine

d.) Hashish

318. Alkaline beam Test performed for detection of:

a.) Dhatura

b.) Arsenic

c.) Morphine

d.) Hashish

319. Odor of rotten eggs is a characteristic odor of which gaseous poison?

a.) Carbon Monoxide

b.) Hydrogen Sulphide

c.) Ammonia

d.) Sulphur dioxide

320. Odor of decaying fish is a characteristic odor of which gaseous poison?

a.) Carbon Monoxide

b.) Hydrogen Sulphide

c.) Phosphine

d.) Sulphur dioxide

321. Odor of Shoe Polish is a characteristic odor of which poison?

a.) Nitrobenzene

b.) Hydrogen Sulphide

c.) Ammonia

d.) Sulphur dioxide

322. Odor of Coal Gas is characteristic odor of which poison?

a.) Malathion

b.) Hydrogen Sulphide

c.) Ammonia

d.) Sulphur dioxide

323. Odor of Garlic is characteristic odor of these poisons, Except:

a.) Malathion

b.) Arsenic

c.) Sulphur dioxide

d.) Parathion

324. Which one of the following poison smell like Freshly Mown Hey?

a.) Sulfur Di-Oxide

b.) Phosgene

c.) Isopropanol

d.) Lewisite

325. When Hydrochloric Acid combined with certain oxidizing chemicals, it can turns into following toxic gas that may cause harm to the skin, eyes and respiratory system:

a.) Carbon Monoxide

b.) Chlorine

c.) Hydrogen Sulphide

d.) Phosphine

326. Which one of the following is use into a wide variety of plastic products, lubricating oils, nail polish, hair spray, etc., and their consumption may cause serious health issues?

a.) Propane

b.) Ethane

c.) Phthalates

d.) Chlorine

327. Which gaseous poison converts Methemoglobin to Sulphametemoglobin?

a.) Carbon Monoxide

b.) Hydrogen Sulphide

c.) Phosphine

d.) Chlorine

328. Prussian blue is Anti-dote for:

a.) Mercury

b.) Thalliium

c.) Arsenic

d.) Lead

329. Calcium Gluconate or edenate is Anti-dote for:

a.) Mercury

b.) Antimony

c.) Magnesium Sulfate

d.) Lead

330. Vomited matter is blue or green turns to deep blue on adding ammonia solution in poisoning from:

a.) Copper

b.) Antimony

c.) Arsenic

d.) Lead

331. In Reinsch Test Purple-Black color is observed which indicates the presence of:

a.) Arsenic

b.) Antimony

c.) Mercury

d.) Thallium

332. Apple Green Flame observed in Flame test which indicates the presence of:

a.) Arsenic

b.) Antimony

c.) Barium

d.) Thallium

333. A Shiny Black deposit on the Copper strip in Reinsch Test indicates the presence of:

a.) Bismuth

b.) Antimony

c.) Mercury

d.) Thallium

334. If Turmeric Paper Strip turns red; following poison is present:

a.) Arsenic

b.) Cadmium

c.) Boric Acid

d.) Acetic Acid

335. In test with Hydrogen Sulphide Yellow precipitate indicates the presence of:

a.) Arsenic

b.) Cadmium

c.) Mercury

d.) Thallium

336. A bright pink spot surrounded by blue circle produced in Test with Dinitro-P-Diphenyl Carbazide indicates the presence of:

a.) Arsenic

b.) Cadmium

c.) Mercury

d.) Thallium

337. In Chemical tests for Chromium following color produced:

a.) Red

b.) Yellow

c.) Black

d.) Brown

338. In Iron poisoning, bloody vomiting and diarrhea, massive fluid loss in GIT, renal failure and death occur in:

a.) Stage I

b.) Stage II

c.) Stage III

d.) Stage IV

339. Shining Silvery deposit on copper are observed in Reinsch Test indicates the presence of:

a.) Arsenic

b.) Mercury

c.) Chromium

d.) Manganese

340. A green color observed in urotropine test, following compound is present:

a.) Strychnine

b.) Brucine

c.) Opium Alkaloids

d.) Cannabis Sativa

341. Test with Lead Acetate produce Golden yellow plates which indicates the presence of:

a.) Flavonoid

b.) Barium

c.) Chromium

d.) Arsenic

342. Nitrogen-Phosphorus Detector (NPD) is used to detect_____:

a.) Pesticides

b.) Volatile poison

c.) Gaseous poison

d.) Metals

343. The dried LSD in long wavelength UV will produced:

a.) Red Color

b.) Blue Fluorescence

c.) Purple Color

d.) Yellow

344. Extract + Marquis develop violet color which indicates the presence of:

a.) Morphine

b.) Codein

c.) Charas

d.) Heroin

345. Extract + Conc. Nitric Acid (HNO$_3$) develop bright Orange Yellow color which indicates the presence of:

a.) Morphine

b.) Codeine

c.) Charas

d.) Heroin

346. Extract + Mandelin's develop Dark Reddish Brown color which indicates the presence of:

a.) Morphine

b.) Codeine

c.) Charas

d.) Heroin

347. Extract + Marquis develop Reddish Purple color which indicates the presence of:

a.) Morphine

b.) Codeine

c.) Charas

d.) Heroin

348. Extract + Conc. Nitric Acid (HNO$_3$) develop Pale Yellow color which indicates the presence of:

a.) Morphine

b.) Codeine

c.) Charas

d.) Heroin

349. Extract + Mandelin's develop Reddish Brown color which indicates the presence of:

a.) Morphine

b.) Codeine

c.) Charas

d.) Heroin

350. Extract + Marquis develop Dark Violet color which indicates the presence of:

a.) Morphine

b.) Codeine

c.) Charas

d.) Heroin

351. Extract + Conc. Nitric Acid (HNO₃) develop Greenish Yellow color which indicates the presence of:

a.) Morphine

b.) Codeine

c.) Charas

d.) Heroin

352. Extract + Mandelin's develop Olive Green color which indicates the presence of:

a.) Morphine

b.) Codeine

c.) Charas

d.) Heroin

353. Extract + Marquis Reagent develop Yellow/Orange color which indicates the presence of:

a.) Benzodiazepines

b.) Alkaloids

c.) Methaqualone

d.) Phenothiazines

354. Extract + FPN Reagent develop Orange red/violet red/Blue color which indicates the presence of:

a.) Benzodiazepines

b.) Alkaloids

c.) Methaqualone

d.) Phenothiazines

355. In McNally's Test a red color formed if _____ is present.

a.) Salicylic Acid

b.) Barbiturates

c.) Phenol

d.) Aspirin

356. Salicylic acid as a medication is used in following disease-

a.) Mental illness

b.) Cancer

c.) Skin disease

d.) All of the above

357. **Keshan disease is a condition caused by deficiency of the following mineral:**

a.) Selenium

b.) Polonium

c.) Thallium

d.) Barium

358. **Neurotic Plant Poison is:**

a.) Strychnos Nux Vomica

b.) Papaver Somniferum

c.) Nicotiana Tabacum

d.) Ergot

359. **Spinal Plant Poison is:**

a.) Strychnos Nux Vomica

b.) Papaver Somniferum

c.) Nicotiana Tabacum

d.) Taxus baccata

360. **Cerebral Plant Poison is:**

a.) Strychnos Nux Vomica

b.) Papaver Somniferum

c.) Nicotiana Tabacum

d.) Cannabis Indica

361. Cardiac Plant Poison is:

a.) Strychnos Nux Vomica

b.) Papaver Somniferum

c.) Nicotiana Tabacum

d.) Cannabis Sativa

362. Irritant Plant Poison is:

a.) Strychnos Nux Vomica

b.) Abrus Precatorius

c.) Nicotiana Tabacum

d.) Cannabis Sativa

363. What's the name of the poison found in deadly nightshades, which is also used in eye surgery?

a.) Atropin

b.) Ricin

c.) Capsaicin

d.) Scopolamine

364. What is a common treatment in case of ingestion of the toxic oleander plant?

a.) Antibiotics

b.) Vomiting

c.) Stomach Pumping

d.) Bulky foods

365. Fatal period of Cannabis Sativa:

a.) 1-2 hours

b.) 3-4 hours

c.) 5 hours

d.) Hours to days

366. Fatal period of Narium Odorum also known as White Oleander (Kaner):

a.) 5-15 min

b.) 1-2 hours

c.) 24-36 hours

d.) 4-5 hours

367. Dile-Koppanyi test for Barbiturates gives color:

a.) Red

b.) Black

c.) Purple

d.) Yellow

368. Which one of the following pairs of drug and indication is accurate:

a.) Amhetamine:Alzheimer's dementia

b.) Bupropion:Acute anxiety

c.) Fluxetine:Insomania

d.) Ropinirole:Parkinson's Disease

369. Which of the following dermatologic findings and potential causes is incorrect?

a.) Cyanosis – Methemoglobinemia

b.) Erythroderma – Boric Acid

c.) Pallor – Carbon Monoxide

d.) Jaundice – Hypercarotinemia (excess carrot intake)

370. Both hepatic and renal toxicity can be caused by :

a.) CCl_4

b.) Arsenic

c.) Copper sulphate

d.) All of the above

371. In treatment of corrosive poisoning, which of the following is not used?

a.) Antacids

b.) Intravenous Fluid

c.) Bulky food

d.) Gastric Lavage

372. Gastric Lavage is contraindicated in poisoning with:

a.) Organophosphorus Compounds

b.) Arsenic

c.) Barbiturates

d.) Sulphuric Acid

373. Sulphuric acid is:

a.) Hygroscopic

b.) Hydroscopic

c.) Both a & b

d.) None of the above

374. Lethal dose of Camphor for adult is:

a.) 4-6 gm

b.) 2 gm

c.) 1 gm

d.) 0.4gm

375. Which of the following poison retard putrefaction?

a.) Organophosphorus

b.) Carbolic Acid

c.) Oxalic Acid

d.) Hydrochloric Acid

376. Glass blowers shakes are seen in poisoning due to:

a.) Arsenic

b.) Mercury

c.) Lead

d.) Copper

377. Mercury affect this part of Kidney:

a.) PCT

b.) Loop of Henle

c.) DCT

d.) Collection duct

378. Average Fatal Period of Copper Poisoning:

a.) 4 hrs

b.) 24-48 hours

c.) 18-36 hours

d.) Hours to Days

379. Toxic Substance commonly used by washer men to put marks on clothes:

a.) Croton tiglium

b.) Semecarpusanacardium

c.) Plumbagorosea

d.) Calotopisprocera.

380. Which of the following snake is poisonous:

a.) Krait

b.) Cobra

c.) Black Mamba

d.) All of the above

381. Cobra poison is :

a.) Myotoxic

b.) Neurotoxic

c.) Cardiotoxic

d.) Hemotoxic

382. Krait poison is :

a.) Myotoxic

b.) Neurotoxic

c.) Cardiotoxic

d.) Hemotoxic

383. Viper snake poison is :

a.) Myotoxic

b.) Neurotoxic

c.) Cardiotoxic

d.) Hemotoxic

384. Venom of sea snake is mostly

a.) Myotoxic

b.) Neurotoxic

c.) Cardiotoxic

d.) Hemotoxic

385. A toxalbumin similar to viperine snake venom is present in the seeds of:

a.) Dhatura

b.) Abrus Precatorius

c.) Ergot

d.) Cannabis

386. The study of Poisoning of Human and Animals by plant is known as:

a.) Plant Toxicology

b.) Toxicology

c.) Forensic Plantology

d.) Phytotoxicology

387. Ophotoxemia refers to:

a.) Organophosphorous poisoning

b.) Scorpion venom poisoning

c.) Snake venom poisoning

d.) Heavy metal poisoning

388. The most useful bedside test to suggest snake bite envenomation is:

a.) Platelet count

b.) 20 min whole blood clotting time

c.) Prothrombin time

d.) International normalized ratio

389. The use of antitoxin in the treatment of snakebite is an example of:

a.) Synergism

b.) Medical Treatment

c.) Chemical Antagonism

d.) Functional Antagonism

390. Which of the following snake is non-poisoning snake?

a.) Viper

b.) Krait

c.) Cobra

d.) Rat snake

391. Which pain relieving drug should be avoided in snake bite poisoning?

a.) Tramadol

b.) Morphine

c.) Aspirin

d.) Paracetamol

392. Narcotic drugs are categorized as:

a.) Antibiotics

b.) Anti-inflammatory

c.) Analgesics

d.) Poisonous Substance

393. When a drug user adheres to the regular schedule of drug intake then he develops:

a.) Withdrawal Sickness

b.) Abstinence Syndrome

c.) Mental Sickness

d.) Physical Dependency

394. Which of the following is not a side effect of Digoxin?

a.) Bradycardia

b.) Yellow vision changes

c.) Scooping of the T segment on ECG

d.) Hypokalemia

395. Substances, which reduce arousal and stimulation is known as:

a.) Depressants

b.) Barbiturates

c.) Hallucinogens

d.) Narcotic Drugs

396. Heroin is made by reacting morphine with:

a.) Ethyl Alcohol

b.) Methyl Alcohol

c.) Acetic Acid

d.) Acetic Anhydride

397. Which is considered as synthetic opiates?

a.) Morphine

b.) Codeine

c.) Heroine

d.) Methadone

398. All are characteristic features of Acute Morphine Poisoning, Except:

a.) Pinpoint Pupil

b.) Low Blood Pressure

c.) Slow labored Breathing

d.) Hyperpyrexia

399. Ganja is obtained from which part of the cannabis plant?

a.) Resin

b.) Flower Top

c.) Leaf

d.) Fruits

400. A potent form of Marijuana is known as:

a.) Coca derivatives

b.) THC

c.) Sinsemilla

d.) Hashish

401. The active components of cannabis responsible for its hallucinogenic properties are the:

a.) Cannabinols

b.) TetrahydroCannabis (THCs)

c.) Tetrahydrocannabinols (THCs).

d.) Tetrahallucinogeniccannabinols (THCs)

402. THCs is:

a.) An Alkaline

b.) Acidic Substance

c.) A fat soluble oleoresin

d.) Derivative

403. Which form of cannabis has the highest concentration of THCs?

a.) Heroin

b.) Cannabis Oil

c.) Methadone

d.) Hashish

404. Which one of the following drug of abuse is over 100 to 300 times more potent than morphine?

a.) Fentanyl

b.) Psilocybe

c.) Mescaline

d.) Mandrex

405. Ethylene Glycol in Antifreeze, first Affects:

a.) Brain

b.) Kidney

c.) Liver

d.) Central Nervous System

406. The Duquenois-levine test is a color test for:

a.) Barbiturates

b.) Marijuana

c.) Acidic Poison

d.) Alcohol

407. Growing substance to suggest that nicotine has its effects by:

a.) Releasing Serotonin into the Cerebellum

b.) Releasing GABA into the hypothalamus

c.) Releasing Dopamine in mesolimbic system of the brain

d.) Releasing Acetykholine into the Diencephalons

408. LSD Full form:

a.) Lysergic Acid Diethylamide

b.) Lysergic Alkali Diethylamide

c.) Lysergic Strychnine Diethylamide

d.) Lysergic Acid Disulphide

409. The effect if LSD was first described by

a.) Adolf Bare

b.) Albert Holfmann

c.) Aristotle

d.) Charak

410. Mixture of PCP(Phencyclidine) and Lysergic Acid Diethylamide is known as:

a.) Narcotic Drug

b.) Weed

c.) Angel Dust

d.) Crack

411. Crack is a term used for:

a.) Marijuana

b.) Barbituric Acid

c.) Amphetamine

d.) Cocaine

412. Speedballs is a combination of heroin and?

a.) Cocaine

b.) Codeine

c.) Thebaine

d.) Papaverine

413. Barbiturates are the derivatives of :

a.) Marijuana

b.) Barbituric Acid

c.) Lysergic Acid

d.) Alcohol

414. Barbiturates was first synthesized by:

a.) Adolf Von Baeyer

b.) Albert Hofmann

c.) Aristotle

d.) Charak

415. Which one is a long acting barbiturate?

a.) Barbital

b.) Phenobarbital

c.) Pentobarbital

d.) Amobarbital

416. In which poisoning color of urine appears Liquid Gold?

a.) Arsenic

b.) Mercury

c.) Barbiturates

d.) Phosphorus

417. Which color test turns orange brown in the presence of amphetamines?

a.) Marquis Test

b.) Scott Test

c.) Gutzeit Test

d.) Play of Colors

418. Cocaine is extracted from:

a.) Cannabis Sativa

b.) Opium

c.) Poppy straw

d.) Erythroxylum coca

419. Cocaine is extracted from which part of Erythroxylum coca?

a.) Stems

b.) Roots

c.) Dried Leaves

d.) Fruits

420. Visual and tactile hallucination with black staining on tongue and teeth is because of:

a.) Heroin

b.) Cannabis Oil

c.) Cocaine

d.) Hashish

421. Feelings of sands under skin or moving insects on skin which cause itching, because of:

a.) Alcohol withdrawal

b.) Morphine Poisoning

c.) Organophosphorus poisoning

d.) Cocaine Poisoning

422. Megnan's Syndrome is seen in case of:

a.) Heroin poisoning

b.) Cocaine Poisoning

c.) Mercury Poisoning

d.) Alcohol Poisoning

423. The most reliable method for estimating blood alcohol level is:

a.) Cavett's Method

b.) Breath analyzer

c.) Thin Layer Chromatography

d.) Gas Liquid Chromatography

424. Which type of poisoning is responsible for Oxalate crystal in urine?

a.) Mercury Poisoning

b.) Arsenic Poisoning

c.) Ethylene Glycol Poisoning

d.) Cocaine Poisoning

425. What specific antidote is used for Ethylene Glycol Poisoning?

a.) Deferoxamine

b.) Bemegride

c.) Penicillamine

d.) Fomepizole

426. Insecticides are a class of:

a.) Volatile Poisons

b.) Non Volatile Poisons

c.) Organic Poisons

d.) Organic Non Volatile Poisons

427. Organophosphorus insecticides are considered as derivatives of:

a.) Phosphonic Acid

b.) Phosphoric Acid

c.) Corresponding Acids

d.) a & b

428. Which of the following is used as a chromogenic spray agent in TLC of Organophosphorus insecticides?

a.) Cobalt acetate-o-toulidine Reagent

b.) Mercurous Nitrate Reagent

c.) Potassium Iodate- starch Reagent

d.) All of the above

429. SLUDGE are symptoms produced by:

a.) Organophosphorus compounds

b.) Carbamates

c.) Organochloro Compound

d.) Barbiturates

430. Stripping is a process used for:

a.) Separation

b.) Absorption

c.) Purification

d.) Cleaning

431. The best specimen for drug and poison screening is:

a.) Blood

b.) Hair

c.) Urine

d.) Nails

432. Sensor Based gas analyzer is used for the extraction of:

a.) Non Volatile Poison

b.) Gaseous Poison

c.) Volatile Organic Poison

d.) Pesticides

433. Electro dialysis digestion is the extraction method for:

a.) Non Volatile Inorganic Poison

b.) Gaseous Poison

c.) Volatile Organic Poison

d.) Pesticides

434. Nestler's Reagent test is Applied for:

a.) Mercury

b.) Chloral Hydrate

c.) Ammonia

d.) Carbon Monoxide

435. Assertion (A): The volatile compounds can be analyzed by GLC.

Reason (R): Because volatile compounds gets precipitated with inert gas in the column.

a.) Both (A) and (R) are correct

b.) Both (A) and (R) are correct but (R) is not the correct explanation of (A)

c.) (A) is False but (R) is True

d.) (A) is True but (R) is False

436. Assertion (A): Ethyl Alcohol forms Metabolite formaldehyde in the body.

Reason (R): Because Formaldehyde is the metabolic end product of Ethyl Alcohol in the body.

a.) Both (A) and (R) are correct

b.) Both (A) and (R) are correct but (R) is not the correct explanation of (A)

c.) (A) is False but (R) is True

d.) (A) is True but (R) is False

437. Match the Scientist With his Findings and Research:

Scientist		Findings
a.) MJB Orfila	(i)	Father of Nerve Agents
b.) Gerhard Schrader	(ii)	Father of Forensic Toxicology
c.) Paul Hermann Muller'	(iii)	Author of 'Silent Spring
d.) Rachel Carson	(iv)	Synthesized DDT

Code:

	(a)	(b)	(c)	(d)
a.)	(i)	(ii)	(iii)	(iv)
b.)	(ii)	(i)	(iv)	(iii)
c.)	(iv)	(iii)	(ii)	(i)
d.)	(iii)	(ii)	(i)	(iv)

438. Match the Following:

List I	List-II
Poison	Actions
a.) Phenol	(i) Deliriant
b.) Dhatura	(ii) Cardiac
c.) Calatropic	(iii) Irritant
d.) Aconite	(iv) Corrosive

Code:

	(a)	(b)	(c)	(d)
a.)	(ii)	(iii)	(iv)	(i)
b.)	(iv)	(i)	(iii)	(ii)
c.)	(iii)	(ii)	(i)	(iv)
d.)	(i)	(iv)	(ii)	(iii)

439. Match the Following Cannabis plant parts on the basis of percentage of THC content find in them.

	List-I	List-II
	Parts	THC %
a.)	Pistillate flower	(i) 1-2%
b.)	Leaves	(ii) 10-12%
c.)	Stalks	(iii) 0.1-0.3%
d.)	Roots	(iv) <0.03%

Code:

	(a)	(b)	(c)	(d)
a.)	(vi)	(i)	(ii)	(iii)
b.)	(iii)	(ii)	(i)	(iv)
c.)	(ii)	(i)	(iii)	(iv)
d.)	(i)	(iv)	(ii)	(iii)

440. Disulfiram is used for treatment of chronic alcohol abuse acts by:

a.) Increasing the concentration of acetaldehyde

b.) Blocking aldehyde dehydrogenase

c.) Blocking acetate dehydrogenase

d.) a & c

441. Soxhlet extractor was invented by:

a.) Karl Landsteiner

b.) Amboise Pare

c.) Franz Von Soxhlet

d.) Paracelsus

442. In the analysis of Poisons, the sequence of events in chronological order is:

a.) Group tests, Extraction, Tissue Homogenisation and specific tests.

b.) Extraction, Group tests, Tissue Homogenisation and specific tests.

c.) Tissue Homogenisation, Extraction, Group tests, and specific tests.

d.) Extraction, Tissue Homogenisation, Group tests and specific tests.

**443. A 35 year old female was found burnt in the kitchen. An empty can of kerosene with little quantity at bottom was found nearby. Match box and few sticks were found on the parapet. She has sustained 100% burns. Black soot was present on the body. Smell of kerosene was observed. Pugilistic attitude was present. Burns from superficial to deep were present on the body. Soot particle were present in trachea. Carboxyhaemoglobin of 15% concentration was reported on analysis. No evidence of mechanical injuries was observed on the body. The room was bolted from the inside. The cause of death was:

a.) Carbon Monoxide Poisoning

b.) Postmortem Burns

c.) Asphyxia due to soot

d.) Antemortem burns

444. Chloral hydrate comes under the following category:

a.) Tranquilizer

b.) Hypnotic

c.) Hallucinogen

d.) Analgesic

445. Quantitative estimation of ethyl alcohol can be done properly in:

a.) Urine

b.) Blood

c.) Saliva

d.) a & b

Forensic Toxicology

446. Ethanol is produced by the fermentation of sugar by:

a.) Yeast

b.) Glycerine

c.) Yoghurt

d.) Alkaloid

447. Which is false?

a.) At pH 7.4 Salicylic Acid is in the unionized form.

b.) When alkalinizing the urine, serum K+ replacement may be required.

c.) Hemodialysis is of benefit.

d.) A serum salicylate level of 2.0 at 6 hours is sufficient for medical discharge.

448. Which of the following term is used to describe the dose of a drug required to kill 50% population under study:

a.) ED99

b.) ED50

c.) LD50

d.) LD1

449. What is the full form of LD50?

a.) Lethal Dose 50

b.) Legal Death 50

c.) Lysergic Dose 50

d.) Least Dose 50

450. Which is true about the LD50?

a.) Dose of a substance to which 50% of Population do not show any response.

b.) Dose of a substance which kills 50% of Population exposed.

c.) 50% of the dose of a substance which can kill Population.

d.) 50 mg/kg dose of a substance to test the toxic responses in Population.

451. Organic mercury targets_____ whereas inorganic mercury primarily targets_____.

a.) Bones, ligaments

b.) Nervous system, kidneys

c.) Hematopoietic system, nervous system

d.) Liver, nervous system

452. 1 ppm is equivalent to:

a.) 1 g/kg

b.) 1 µg/kg

c.) 1 mg/kg

d.) 1 mg/100g

453. Which Scientist suggested the use of Palatal rugae for identity verification:

a.) Harrison Allen

b.) Ambroise Pare

c.) Arstotle

d.) 1 mg/100g

454. Which is the wrong mechanism of action for the listed drug/toxin?

a.) Colchicine: binds to intracellular tubulin preventing cell mitosis

b.) Amanita phalloides: impairs DNA synthesis

c.) Strychnine: inhibits glycine in the spinal cord

d.) Isoniazid: reduces folate activity

455. Which of the following is use in Molotov cocktail?

a.) Gasoline

b.) Magnesium

c.) Arsenic

d.) Mercury

456. Which of the following is not an Insecticide?

a.) Fluoroacetamide

b.) Malachite green

c.) Nicotine

d.) Malathion

457. Which Liquid poison is considered a dangerous chemical due to its extremely foul odor? This is also known as smelliest chemical.

a.) Cadaverine

b.) Butyric acid

c.) Thioacetone

d.) Ethyl Mercaptan

458. Thioacetone is dangerous because:

a.) It is explosive

b.) It is flammable

c.) It has worst smell

d.) All of the above

459. These are Blood agents, Except:

a.) Hydrogen Cyanide

b.) Arsine

c.) Cyanogen

d.) Sarin

460. This blood agent also act as a choking agent:

a.) Hydrogen Cyanide

b.) Phosgene

c.) Arsine

d.) Cyanogen

461. This blood agent also act as a Blister agent:

a.) Hydrogen Cyanide

b.) Phosgene

c.) Vinyl Arsine

d.) Cyanogen

462. Each of the following statement is true about Oxalic Acid, Except:

a.) It is Corrosive

b.) It may contribute to kidney stones

c.) Large exposures may lead to pulmonary edema

d.) Ingestion of soluble oxalates is not harmful

463. Which statement is false?

a.) VX is odorless and tasteless.

b.) Production of Thioacetone led to the evacuation of the German city of Freiburg in 1889.

c.) Very short contact with fumes or small quantities of the liquid of Hydrogen Fluoride can cause severe, painful burns.

d.) There is no Antidote for Nerve Agents.

464. Which of the following toxins is not produced by bacteria?

a.) Cholera toxin

b.) Aflatoxin

c.) Botulinum toxin

d.) Diphtheria toxin

465. Ergotism is associated with toxin produced by _____:

a.) Plant

b.) Fungus

c.) Virus

d.) Mycoplasma

466. Aspergillus species produce Aflatoxins, Aflatoxin B1. One of the aflatoxins causes following toxic effects in humans:

a.) Severe liver toxicity and Carcinogenesis

b.) It is less toxic due to its natural origin

c.) Cardiotoxicity

d.) Respiratory collapse

467. Tetrodotoxin, a deadly toxin, is found in _____:

a.) Rattle snake

b.) Mussels

c.) Puffer fish

d.) Scorpion

468. Which is the most likely toxic effect of cosmetics?

a.) Skin corrosion

b.) Allergic contact dermatitis

c.) Local muscular degeneration

d.) Major risk of systemic toxicity after absorption of

469. Gastrointestinal tract does not have any profound effect on nature of ingested chemicals:

a.) True

b.) False

c.) Gut-microflora plays important role in biotransformation of ingested chemicals

d.) It does not matter whether gastrointestinal tract have any effects on chemicals

470. Which of the following is the main way of transportation of a lipid soluble toxicant within body?

a.) Filtration

b.) Endocytosis

c.) a & b

d.) Passive diffusion

471. What is the most common toxicity target of ethanol (beverage alcohol) in humans?

a.) Fetus

b.) Liver

c.) Kidneys

d.) Heart

472. What are the common targets of ethanol toxicity in humans?

a.) Liver, brain, heart and kidneys

b.) Liver, lungs and intestine

c.) Liver, brain and fetus

d.) Spleen, liver, brain and thymus

473. Which part of the body is primarily affected by caffeine intoxication?

a.) Heart

b.) Brain

c.) Liver

d.) Kidneys

474. Leaves from the following plants are the significant source of caffeine.

a.) Coffea arabica

b.) Erythroxylum coca

c.) Cola acuminata

d.) Camellia sinensis

475. Exposure to _____ is associated with occupation.

a.) Aflatoxins

b.) Formaldehyde

c.) Ethanol

d.) Acetaminophen

476. Exposure to _____ is associated with lifestyle.

a.) Chromium

b.) Benzidine

c.) Nicotine

d.) Asbestos

477. Which statements is true regarding GHB (gamma hydroxybutyrate)?

a.) Is a psychoactive drug of abuse

b.) It has been used clinically to treat narcolepsy, as an anesthetic agent, to treat alcohol withdrawal and in body building.

c.) It has a very short elimination half-life (30 mins) and thus may not be detectable in a urine sample taken after delay of several hours.

d.) All of the above

478. _____ is a most widely used Rodenticides and Pesticides.

a.) Brodifacoum

b.) Tetradotoxin

c.) Batrachotoxin

d.) All of the above

479. Which statement is false about Lithium toxicity?

a.) Toxicity associated with chronic use occurs at lower serum levels

b.) In a non-user an acute overdose may not be symptomatic until the serum level is greater than 3

c.) Most effects of acute OD are neurological

d.) Appropriate management of an acute OD could include charcoal, IV fluids and haemodialysis

480. Repeated High exposure of _____ to the body can lead to bone disease.

a.) Chromium

b.) Benzidine

c.) Nicotine

d.) Sodium Fluoride

481. With regard to snake bite which is true?

a.) There is no specific sea snake antivenom.

b.) Tiger and brown snakes are more less likely to cause paralysis than black snake.

c.) The dose of antivenom needed for tiger snake envenomation is usually one vial.

d.) The antivenom should be diluted 1in 10 in normal saline and given over half an hour.

482. Comparing the Red-Back and the Funnel Web Spiders, which is false?

a.) Female Red-back and Male Funnel Web are harmful.

b.) Death due to the bite from Funnel Web Spider can happen within 15min-1hour.

c.) The Red-Back Spider venom is rabbit based and given with little risk of allergy.

d.) Severe toxicity with Red-Back Spider envenomation takes at least three hours.

483. Kim Jong-Nam (half-brother of Kim Jong-Un, who is currently leader of North Korea) was killed by spray of this poison:

a.) Trimethylamine Oxide

b.) Hydrogn Selenide

c.) VX

d.) None of the above

484. Trimethylamine oxide is found in_____:

a.) Marine Fish

b.) Snakes

c.) Bacteria

d.) All of the above

485. What does Hydrogen Selenide Smell like?

a.) Rotten fish

b.) Mustard seeds

c.) Rotten eggs mixed with rotten radishes

d.) Feces

486. Mesothelioma (cancer of lining covering internal organs) is associated with exposure to ____:

a.) Nickel

b.) Mercury

c.) Benzene

d.) Asbestos

487. Asbestos made from?

a.) From naturally occurring fibrous minerals.

b.) From Bacteria.

c.) From Fish.

d.) From Artificial.

488. All statements are true about symptoms of Sulfur Mustard, except:

a.) Sulfur mustard sometimes smells like garlic, onions or mustard and sometimes it has no odor.

b.) Sulfur mustard is naturally in the environment.

c.) Mild respiratory distress to marked airway damage.

d.) Exposure to sulfur mustard usually is not fatal.

489. Which gas was leaked in Bhopal gas Tragedy in 1984?

a.) Carbon monoxide

b.) Hydrocyanic acid

c.) Methyl Isocyanate

d.) Styrene Gas

490. Which gas was leaked in Vizag (Visakhapatnam) gas Tragedy in 2020?

a.) Carbon monoxide

b.) Hydrocyanic acid

c.) Methyl Isocyanate

d.) Styrene Gas

491. One of the following method is best to avoid aspiration of fluids during gastric lavage in a comatose patient:

a.) Introduction of a cuffed endotracheal tube before lavage

b.) Keeping the head of the patient at a lower level than his feet

c.) Putting the patient in the left lateral position

d.) Continuous suction of the fluid from the trachea

492. Heneicosane is a characteristic component of which of the following?

a.) Kerosene

b.) Petrol

c.) Diesel

d.) Oils

493. Pristane and phytane are present only in which of the following?

a.) Heavy Petroleum Distillate

b.) Medium Petroleum Distillate

c.) Light Petroleum Distillate

d.) Gasoline

494. Gastric lavage turned black when it was healed after being treated with silver nitrate, this can be seen in following poisoning:

a.) Parathion

b.) Malathion

c.) Celphos

d.) Arsenic

495. Sui/Sitari are prepared from:

a.) Croton Tiglium

b.) Cannabis sativa

c.) Abrus Precatorius

d.) Morphine

496. Priapism occurs in:

a.) Cantharides

b.) Phosphorus

c.) Mercury

d.) a & b

497. "Ewing's postulate" refers to:

a.) Relationship between Trauma and Tumor

b.) Complications result from trauma

c.) The role of disease in modifying the effects of trauma

d.) Congenital abnormalities caused by drugs

498. Reed's classification is use for:

a.) Grade of dead body

b.) Grade of toxicity

c.) Grade of loss of consciousness

d.) Grade of loss of blood

499. Prolonged Prothrombin time occurs in cases of poisoning with:

a.) Thallium

b.) Thioacetone

c.) Warfarin

d.) Hydrocyanic acid

500. New born is more sensitive to following toxicity than an adult:

a.) DDT

b.) Lead

c.) Malathion

d.) b & c

Answer-Sheet

MCQs on Forensic Toxicology

1	b	2	c	3	d	4	a	5	b
6	d	7	a	8	a	9	d	10	b
11	c	12	b	13	a	14	a	15	c
16	d	17	c	18	d	19	c	20	a
21	d	22	c	23	d	24	a	25	d
26	b	27	f	28	b	29	e	30	b
31	b	32	d	33	d	34	d	35	c
36	c	37	c	38	e	39	d	40	c
41	b	42	d	43	b	44	b	45	a
46	d	47	b	48	a	49	a	50	d
51	c	52	c	53	a	54	b	55	c
56	a	57	c	58	a	59	b	60	d
61	d	62	b	63	a	64	b	65	a
66	d	67	b	68	a	69	d	70	c
71	c	72	a	73	c	74	c	75	a
76	c	77	c	78	a	79	c	80	b
81	a	82	d	83	c	84	a	85	d
86	b	87	a	88	c	89	b	90	d
91	c	92	a	93	d	94	c	95	a
96	c	97	a	98	c	99	b	100	d

MCQs on Forensic Toxicology

101	d	102	a	103	c	104	b	105	c
106	d	107	a	108	b	109	d	110	a
111	b	112	a	113	c	114	c	115	d
116	b	117	d	118	c	119	a	120	d
121	d	122	b	123	d	124	a	125	c
126	d	127	d	128	a	129	d	130	b
131	a	132	b	133	c	134	d	135	c
136	c	137	a	138	c	139	a	140	a
141	d	142	b	143	c	144	c	145	c
146	b	147	c	148	a	149	b	150	c
151	d	152	a	153	e	154	c	155	d
156	c	157	c	158	d	159	a	160	c
161	b	162	a	163	b	164	d	165	d
166	a	167	c	168	d	169	d	170	b
171	d	172	b	173	a	174	c	175	c
176	b	177	c	178	a	179	d	180	b
181	d	182	a	183	c	184	a	185	d
186	d	187	a	188	a	189	c	190	a
191	c	192	b	193	c	194	d	195	a
196	b	197	b	198	a	199	c	200	d

MCQs on Forensic Toxicology

201	b	202	a	203	b	204	b	205	d
206	a	207	c	208	a	209	c	210	c
211	a	212	b	213	b	214	a	215	c
216	b	217	c	218	b	219	d	220	d
221	c	222	d	223	b	224	c	225	b
226	d	227	a	228	d	229	b	230	a
231	b	232	c	233	b	234	d	235	c
236	b	237	a	238	b	239	d	240	b
241	c	242	b	243	d	244	b	245	b
246	b	247	c	248	b	249	c	250	a
251	a	252	b	253	c	254	b	255	a
256	d	257	a	258	d	259	a	260	b
261	d	262	d	263	d	264	b	265	e
266	b	267	a	268	d	269	d	270	a
271	d	272	c	273	c	274	d	275	b
276	a	277	d	278	a	279	b	280	a
281	d	282	a	283	b	284	a	285	b
286	a	287	b	288	d	289	a	290	a
291	b	292	a	293	c	294	d	295	a
296	d	297	c	298	c	299	b	300	c

301	b	302	c	303	d	304	c	305	b
306	c	307	d	308	c	309	a	310	d
311	b	312	b	313	c	314	b	315	d
316	a	317	a	318	d	319	b	320	c
321	a	322	d	323	c	324	d	325	b
326	c	327	b	328	b	329	c	330	a
331	b	332	c	333	a	334	c	335	b
336	b	337	a	338	a	339	b	340	c
341	a	342	a	343	b	344	a	345	a
346	a	347	d	348	d	349	d	350	b
351	b	352	b	353	a	354	d	355	a
356	c	357	a	358	b	359	a	360	d
361	c	362	b	363	a	364	c	365	d
366	c	367	c	368	d	369	c	370	d
371	d	372	d	373	a	374	a	375	b
376	b	377	a	378	c	379	b	380	d
381	b	382	b	383	d	384	a	385	b
386	d	387	c	388	b	389	c	390	d
391	c	392	c	393	d	394	d	395	a
396	d	397	d	398	d	399	b	400	d

MCQs on Forensic Toxicology

401	c	402	c	403	b	404	a	405	d
406	b	407	c	408	a	409	b	410	c
411	d	412	a	413	b	414	a	415	b
416	c	417	a	418	d	419	c	420	c
421	d	422	b	423	d	424	c	425	d
426	d	427	d	428	d	429	a	430	c
431	c	432	b	433	a	434	c	435	b
436	b	437	b	438	b	439	c	440	d
441	c	442	c	443	a	444	b	445	d
446	a	447	d	448	c	449	a	450	b
451	b	452	c	453	a	454	d	455	a
456	b	457	c	458	c	459	d	460	b
461	c	462	d	463	d	464	b	465	b
466	a	467	c	468	b	469	c	470	d
471	b	472	c	473	b	474	d	475	b
476	c	477	d	478	a	479	d	480	d
481	d	482	c	483	c	484	a	485	c
486	d	487	a	488	b	489	c	490	d
491	a	492	c	493	a	494	c	495	c
496	d	497	a	498	c	499	c	500	d

BIBLIOGRAPHY AND SUGGESTED READING

- Some questions have been taken from different competitive examinations question papers.

- The Merck Veterinary Manual (2016). Chapter "Herbicide Poisoning" by PK GUPTA 11th edition, Merck & Co. Inc Whitehouse Station, NJ, USA 2969-99

- *Textbook of Forensic Medicine and Toxicology, V. V. Pillay, 14th edition, p369.*

- Gupta PK (2016) Essential Concepts in Toxicology. Published by PharmaMed Press (A unit of BSP Books Pvt. Ltd), Hyderabad, India pp 362

- Anderson, M. E., R. S. Thomas, K. W. Gaido, et al. Dose - response modeling in reproductive toxicology in the systems biology era. *Reprod. Toxicol.* 19 : 327 – 337 , 2005.

- Deighton, N. Metabolomics. In *Molecular and Biochemical Toxicology,* eds. R. C. Smart and E. Hodgson, pp. 67 – 79. Hoboken, NJ: Wiley, 2008.

- Edwards, S. W. and R. J. Preston. Systems biology and mode of action based risk assessment. *Toxically. Sci.* 106: 312 – 318, 2008.

- Harrill, A. H., P. K. Ross, D. M. Gatti, et al. Population - based discovery of toxicogenomics biomarkers for hepatotoxicity using a laboratory strain diversity panel. *Toxicol.Sci.* 110: 235 – 243, 2009.

- Merrick, B. A. Proteomics. In *Molecular and Biochemical Toxicology,* eds. R. C. Smart and E. Hodgson, pp. 41 – 66. Hoboken, NJ: Wiley, 2008.

- National Research Council. Toxicity testing in the 21st century: A vision and a strategy.

- Washington, DC: National Research Council Committee on Toxicity Testing and Assessment of Environmental Agents, National Academy Press, 2007.

- Olelsiak, M. F. Toxicogenomics. In *Molecular and Biochemical Toxicology,* eds. R. C. Smart and E. Hodgson, pp. 25 – 39. Hoboken, NJ: Wiley, 2008.

- Plant, N. Can systems toxicology identify common biomarkers of non - genotoxic carcinogenesis? *Toxicology* 254: 164 – 169, 2008.

- Smart, R. C. and E. Hodgson, eds. *Molecular and Biochemical Toxicology.* Hoboken, NJ: John Wiley and Sons, 2008.

- Stone, E. A. and D. M. Nielsen. Bioinformatics. In *Molecular and Biochemical Toxicology,* eds.

- R. C. Smart and E. Hodgson, pp. 81 – 107. Hoboken, NJ: Wiley, 2008.

- Waring , J. F. , R. Ciurlionis , R. A. Jolly , et al. Microarray analysis of hepatotoxins in vitro reveals a correlation between gene expression profile les and mechanisms of toxicity . *Toxicol.Lett.* 120: 359 – 368, 2001.

- Joy, R. M. Neurotoxicology: Central and peripheral. In *Encyclopedia of Toxicology,* vol. 2,P. Wexler, ed. New York: Academic Press, 1998, pp. 389–413.

- Stryer, L. *Biochemistry,* 4th ed. San Francisco: W. H. Freeman, 1999.

- Eaton, D. L., and C. D. Klaassen. Principles of toxicology In *Casarrett and Doull's Toxicology: The Basic Science of Poisons,* 6th ed. C. D. Klaassen, ed. New York: McGraw-Hill, 2001, pp.11–34.

- Calabrese, E. J., and L. A. Baldwin. U-shaped dose-responses in biology, toxicology, and publichealth. *An. Rev. Public Health* 22: 15–33, 2001.

- Bondar, V. S. Toxicological chemistry. Schemes and Tables: Handbook for students of higher schools / V. S. Bondar, S. A. Karpushina. – Kharkiv: NUPh: Golden Pages, 2009. – 120 p.

- Karpushina, S. A. Toxicological chemistry. Lecture course / S. A. Karpushina, V. S. Bondar, I. A. Zhuravel. – Kharkiv: NUPh: Golden pages, 2011. – 208 p.

- Toxicological Chemistry. Laboratory workbook / S. A. Karpushina, I. A. Zhuravel, V. S. Bondar, S. V. Bayurka. – Kharkiv: NUPh, 2012. – 63 p.

- Baselt, C. R. Disposition of Toxic Drugs and Chemicals in Man: 9-th edition / R. C. Baselt. – California: Biomedical Publications, 2011. – 1900 p.

- Basic Analytical Toxicology / R. J. Flanagan [et al.]. – Geneva: World Health organization, 1995. – 363 p.

- Bell, S. Forensic Chemistry / S. Bell. – New Jersey: Pearson Prentice Hall. – 671 p.

- Clarke's analysis of drugs and poisons in pharmaceuticals, body fluids and postmortem material: 4-th edition / A. C. Moffat [et al.]. – London; Chicago: Pharmaceutical Press, 2011. – 2736 p.

- Clarke's Analytical Forensic Toxicology / ed. by Sue Jickells, Adam Negrusz. – London: Pharmaceutical Press, 2008. – 648 p.

- Flanagan, R. J. Developing Analytical Toxicology Services: Principles and Guidance [Electronic resource] / R. J. Flanagan. – Geneva: World Health Organization, 2005. – 36 p. – Available at: http://www.who.int/ipcs/publications/training_poisons/hospitalnalytical_toxicology.pdf (date of the application: (07.09.2017). – Developing Analytical Toxicology Services: Principles and Guidance.

- Gracia RC, Snodgrass WR. Lead toxicity and chelation therapy. Am J Health Syst Pharm. 2007 Jan 1; 64(1):45-53.

- Mann KV, Travers JD. Succimer, an oral lead chelator. Clin Pharm. 1991 Dec; 10(12):914-22.

- Patrick L. Lead toxicity, a review of the literature. Part 1: Exposure, evaluation, and treatment. Altern Med Rev. 2006 Mar; 11(1):2-22.

- Poisoning & Drug Overdose. Fourth Edition / ed. by Kent R. Olson. – Zange Medical Books, Mc Graw-Hill, 2004. – 718 p.

- https://en.wikipedia.org/wiki/History_of_poison.

- Kaviraja Ambikadutta Shastri: Editor, Susrutsamhita of Maharsi-Susruta Edited with AyurvedaTatva-Sandipika, Kalpasthana; Sthavarvish-vidnyaniyam Adhyaya: Chapter 2, Verse 33, Chaukhmba Sanskrit Sansthan Publication, Varanasi, Second Edition, part 1, 2010; 32 [45]

- Udayvir Shastri: Editor, Kautilaya Arthashasrta of Vishnugupta Kautalya Edited with 'Nayachandrika' Hindi Commentry, Volume 2, Ashumrutak Parikshan,Chapter no. 82, Verse 21-30.Bharat Bharti publication, Delhi, Second Edition.1969:135-137.

- https://en.wikipedia.org/wiki/History_of_poison.

- Dr. Parikh C.K, Parikh's Textbook of Medical Jourisprudence Forensic Medicine and Toxicology, Section VIII, Introduction to Toxicology, CBS Publishers & Distributors, Dehli, Sixth Edition Reprint-2007; 8(9).

- Dr. Mathiharan K, Dr. Patnaik AK.Modi's Medical Jurisprudence and Toxicology, Section 2,Diagnosis of Poisoning:Chapter 1,Lexis Nexis Publication, Dehli,Twenty Third Edition, 2006: 21-29

- Dr. U. R. Shekhar Namburi, editor. Agadtantra, Diagnosis of Poisoning, Chapter 05, 1st edition, Chaukhambha Sanskrit Sansthan Varanasi, 2013; 41 & 42.

- Dr. Brahmanand Tripathi, Editor, Charakasamhita of Agnivesha Edited with 'Charak-Chandrika' Hindi Commentary, Volume 2, Chikitsasthana; Vishachikitsaadhyaya, Chapter 23, verse 16, Chaukhmba Surbharati Prakashan, Delhi, Reprint, 2002; 749.

- Kaviraja Ambikadutta Shastri: Editor, Susrutsamhita of Maharsi-Susruta Edited with AyurvedaTatva-Sandipika, Kalpasthana; Sthavarvish-vidnyaniyam Adhyaya: Chapter 1, Verse 42, Chaukhmba Sanskrit Sansthan Publication, Varanasi, Second Edition, part 1, 2010; 08.

- Prof. K. R. Srikant Murthy, editor Ashtanga Sangraha of Vagbhata, Sutrasthana, Annaraksha Vidhi Adhyaya, 8/48, 9th edition, Chaukhmbha Orientalia, Varanasi, 2005; 167.

- Kaviraja Ambikadutta Shastri: Editor, Susrutsamhita of Maharsi-Susruta Edited with AyurvedaTatva-Sandipika, Kalpasthana; Sthavarvish-vidnyaniyam Adhyaya: Chapter 1, Verse 56, Chaukhmba Sanskrit Sansthan Publication, Varanasi, Second Edition, part 1, 2010; 11.

- Dr. Brahmanand Tripathi: Editor, Ashtanghrudayam of Shrimadvagbhata Edited with 'Nirmala Hindi commentary', Uttarasthan; Vishpratishedhadhyay, Chapter 35, Verse, 50-53, Chaukhmba Sanskrit Pratishthan, Delhi: Reprint, 2007; 1150.

- Udayvir Shastri: Editor, Kautilaya Arthashasrta of Vishnugupta Kautalya Edited with 'Nayachandrika' Hindi Commentry, Volume 2, Ashumrutak Parikshan, Chapter no. 82. Bharat Bharti publication, Delhi, Second Edition, 1969; 135-137.

- Dr. Parikh C.K., Parikh's Textbook of Medical Jourisprudence Forensic Medicine and Toxicology, Section 10, Fuels, 52, CBS Publishers & Distributors, Dehli, Sixth Edition Reprint-2007; 10.39.

- Bardale Rajesh, Principles of Forensic Medicine and Toxicology, Section 2, Toxicology:General Considerations:Chapter 33,The Health Science Publishers,Dehli,,Second Editon, 2017; 473-474.

- Dr. Parikh C.K., Parikh's Textbook of Medical Jourisprudence Forensic Medicine and Toxicology,Section VIII, Introduction to Toxicology, CBS Publishers & Distributors, Dehli, Sixth Edition Reprint-2007; 8.11.

- AK Jaiswal, Handbook of Forensic Analytical Toxicology, chapter no.4, Thin Layer Chromatography and its application, 1st edition, Jaypee publication Dehli, 2014; 139.

- http://plato.mercyhurst.edu/chemistry/kjircitano/ChemPrincLaboratories/Drugs.

- AK Jaiswal, Handbook of Forensic Analytical Toxicology, chapter no.5, Thin Layer Chromatography and its application, 1st edition, Jaypee publication Dehli, 2014; 214.

- Dr. Mathiharan K, Dr. Patnaik AK.Modi's Medical Jurisprudence and Toxicology, Section 2, Poisons and their Medicolegal Aspects: Chapter 1,Lexis Nexis Publication, Dehli,Twenty Third Edition, 2006; 29.

- https://www.eolss.net/Sample-Chapters/C09/E6-12-23-00.pdf.

- Blanke RV, Poklis A, Analytic/Forensic Toxicology In: Amdur MO, Doull J, Klaassen CD editors. Cascarett and Doull's Toxicology The Basic Science of Poisons.4th ed. London: Pergamon Press, 1992; 905-923.

- 54. Dr. Mathiharan K, Dr. Patnaik AK., Modi's Medical Jurisprudence and Toxicology, Section 2, Poisons and their Medicolegal Aspects: Chapter 1,Lexis Nexis Publication, Dehli, Twenty Third Edition, 2006; 29.

- http://plato.mercyhurst.edu/chemistry/kjircitano/ChemPrincLaboratories/Drugs.

- AK Jaiswal, Handbook of Forensic Analytical Toxicology, chapter no.12, Breath Alcohol Analyser and its application, 1st edition, Jaypee publication Dehli, 2014; 442-444.

- Broughton, P. M. G. A rapid ultraviolet spectrophotometric method for the detection, estimation and identification of barbiturates in biological material.

- *Biochem. J.* 63 (1956) 207.

- Clarke, E. G. C. (Ed.) *Isolation and Identification 0/ Drugs*(1969) Pharmaceutical Press, London, £14.00.

- Curry. A. S. *Simple Tests to Detect Poisoning. (1966)* Association of Clinical Pathologists Broadsheet No. 52,25p.

- Curry, A. S. *Poison Detection in Human Organs.* 2nd ed.(1969) Thomas, Springfield, £5.78.

- Dauphinais, R. M., McComb, R. A specific procedure for serum glutethimide (Doriden) determination. *Amer.J. C/in. Path.* 44 (1965) 440.

- Forrest, I. S., Forrest, F. M., Mason, A. S. A rapid urine colour test for imipramine (TofraniI, Geigy): supplementary report with colour chart. *Amer. J. Psychiat.* 116 (1960) 1021.

- Forrest, I. S., Forrest, F. M. Urine colour test for the detection of phenothiazine compounds. *C/in. Chem.* 6 (1960) 11.

- Garvey, K., Bowden, C. M. The colorimetric determination of barbiturates. *Proc. Assoc. din. Biochem.* 4 (1966) 20.

- Lawson, A. A. H., Brown, S. S. Acute methaqualone (Mandrax) poisoning. *Scot. med. J-.* 12 (1967) 63.

- Matthew, H., Lawson, A. A. H. *Treatment 0/ Common Acute Poisonings.* 2nd ed. (1970), Livingstone, Edinburgh,£1.00.

- Routh, J. I., Shane, N. A., Arredondo, E. G., Paul, W. D. Determination of N-acetyl-p-aminophtnol in plasma. *C/in. Chem.* 14 (1968) 882.

- Sunshine, I. *Handbook 0/ Analytical Toxicology. (1969)* Chemical Rubber Co., Cleveland, £14'00.

- Sunshine, I., Gerber, S. R. *Spectrophotometric Analysis 0/ Drugs.* Including Atlas of Spectra (1963) Thomas, Springfield, £4.50.

- Todd, R. G. (Ed.) *Extra Pharmacopoeia: Martindale,* 25th ed. (1967) Pharmaceutical Press, London, £7.50.

- Trinder, P. Rapid determination of salicylate in biological fluids. *Biochem. J.* 57 (1954) 301.

- Whitehead, T. P., Worthington, S. The determination of carboxyhaemoglobin. *C/in. chim. Acta* 6 (1961) 356.

- Kanji S, MacLean RD. Cardiac glycoside toxicity: more than 200 years and counting. Crit Care Clin. 2012 Oct; 28(4):527-35.

- Smith TW. Digitalis. Mechanisms of action and clinical use. N Engl J Med. 1988 Feb 11; 318(6):358-65.

- Wright RO et al. Methemoglobinemia: etiology, pharmacology, and clinical management. Ann Emerg Med. 1999 Nov;34(5):646-56.

- Schillinger BM et al. Boric Acid Poisoning. J Am Acad Dermatol. 1982 Nov;7(5):667-73.

- Piantadosi CA. Carbon monoxide poisoning. N Engl J Med. 2002 Oct 3;347(14):1054-5.

- Mazzone A, Dal Canton A. Image in clinical medicine. Hypercarotenemia. N Engl J Med. 2002 Mar 14;346(11):821.

- Hochholzer W. The facts behind niacin. Ther Adv Cardiovasc Dis. 2011 Oct;5(5):227-40.

www.ingramcontent.com/pod-product-compliance
Lightning Source LLC
Chambersburg PA
CBHW072029230526
45466CB00020B/1181